The Possible Woman

*Exploring Feminine
Wisdom, Spirit,
and Potential*

Marjorie Barlow

The Possible Woman

Exploring Feminine Wisdom, Spirit, and Potential

by

Marjorie R. Barlow, Ph.D.

BARLOW
BOOKS

Out of respect for the privacy and confidentiality of
my clients, all references to individuals in this book are
based on composites. Any reference to a specific person is
unintentional and coincidental.

Edited and produced by Phyllis Mueller
Design and typesetting by Studio Supplee
Illustrations by Marilyn King
Author's photo by Reba Graham
Printing by Print Production Management
Printed in the United States of America.

To Dr. Jean Houston –
teacher, mentor, evocateur, friend –
and Melissa Ann Robinson,
my granddaughter,
who represents
the future Possible Woman

This is the short list of those I want to thank. Their contributions to my life are boundless and still continue. I acknowledge the following:

• My parents, Victoria Kiker and Odie McNeely, for their "good genes" and good hearts. They were leaders in their day and made a difference in the lives of those they touched. I deeply appreciate their perseverance during hard times, their dedication to truth as they perceived it, and their adherence to their morality.

• My best friend and my husband, Dr. Paul Barlow, for his belief in me and his support of my becoming myself. He gave his life to me and my first family of four children. He became their father in real truth, offering them adoption in their adulthood. Our fifth child was his opportunity to be a parent from the beginning, and I am deeply grateful for his magnificent fatherhood. He is my partner in our spiritual deepening, my advocate in times of stress, my support in times of need, and a companion in the pursuit of joy and happiness. I acknowledge our love and our desire to grow old together.

• My children, Anna Brown, Michael Robinson, Kaye Barlow, Dr. Edward Robinson, and Cynthia Barlow. They are my love and my life. Without them, I would be a half-light version of myself. Their families are also acknowledged: Janice Brooks Robinson, Lee Michael Robinson, Melissa Ann Robinson, John Brown, Rose Wang, and Debbie Vardell. They provide the rich mix at our family get togethers.

- My teachers – Dr. Jean Houston, Dr. Joyce Buckner, Dr. Muriel James – who have provided the doors to learning. Jean inspired the ideas and actions that became the Possible Woman workshop and book. Her work is evocatory, always positive, and world impacting. Joyce taught me Imago Relationship Theory with diligence and rich experiences. Muriel was my teacher years ago in the theories of transactional analysis and Self Re-Parenting. I appreciated her as a loving sister and warm, caring teacher. Many others have been helpful teachers. These three women especially inspired this book.

- My clients from thirty years of work as a counselor. I had the honor of their trust and the privilege of witnessing changes in each life story. This has been a rich learning experience for me, and I am grateful.

- My lifelong colleagues and friends, LaNelle Ford, Psy.D., Joyce Spindle, Ph.D., Paul Bryant, Ed.D., John Gladfelter, Ph.D., George Kramer, Ph.D., J. Zink, Ph.D., Wilfred Whiteside, D.D.S, and David Stringer, Th.D.

- My current friendly guides: All the members of my Women's Wisdom Group; my colleagues in the Association for Imago Relationship Therapy (especially President Martha Beveridge, A.S.C.W.); Possible Woman Enterprises organizer, Linda Wind; David Oakey and my friends at Pond Studio; and Joyce LaValle of Interface, Inc., who is the classic Possible Woman.

Special thanks go to Paul Barlow and Cynthia Barlow for their able assistance in the early stages of the production of this book. Cynthia is a real computer whiz who can take a manuscript to the form needed for the next step. I appreciate her talent, her skills, and her alacrity. Paul gave the emotional support, the professor's eye, and the real permission to write this book.

Phyllis Mueller, my accomplished editor and book-maker, deserves special appreciation. Phyllis is a student of life as well as a student of women's stories. I needed her encouragement and enthusiasm when I was less than excited about one more re-write and her challenge to me in making my ideas as clear as possible for the reader. Over a period of several months, she took my handcrafted "first edition" of *The Possible Woman* and helped me bring it into new form. I am grateful to her, for without her competence, patience, and optimism, this book would have remained a small edition of lovingly handcrafted, self-assembled books for women.

Phyllis's work was brought to my attention by Charlie Eitel, who was the original benefactor of this work. Although Phyllis had not worked with Charlie on his books, he was aware of her work with other writers. One such is Ray C. Anderson, CEO of **Interface, Incorporated.** Phyllis contributed her editing skills to his timely and important book, *Mid-Course Correction: Toward a Sustainable Enterprise – The Interface Model.* Sustainability and restoration of the resources of planet Earth are the subjects of Ray Anderson's book. I am honored to join with those who are devoted to that vital mission, which requires all of us to reach for a higher level of development as human beings.

Marj Barlow
November 1999
Corpus Christi, Texas

TABLE OF CONTENTS

WELCOME

When I was six months old, I won a contest and was pronounced a Perfect Baby. Recently, I asked my mother how they knew I was perfect. She said, "They weighed and measured you." I asked what that proved and she replied, "You matched the books!" I suggested the books showed average weight and height for a certain age. She said, "It didn't matter. You won the silver spoon."

This is a recurring pattern in my life; all the things that have happened to me seem to have certain patterns to them. Some patterns are good, and some are bad. But I am the common denominator; I am the only one consistently present. If I am to create my life as an answer to the questions "Who am I?" and "What could I be?" then I need to be aware of and take responsibility for the patterns. I compare the patterns to computer generated fractals. The blossoming, unfolding, beautiful shapes appear on the computer screen as different, yet they are based in a mathematical formula. Winning the Perfect Baby Contest was my first fractal. I have a pattern of being average and still winning.

Knowing that a pattern exists helps in understanding my behavior, but I am ultimately responsible for claiming my potential. I have will, volition, and intentionality. I must decide what I want. The potential is there. I can claim it.

What really helps one individual woman to become all she can be? What does woman really want? Who is she? What could she become? These questions and many others are the basis for the pursuit of the Possible Woman, an idea born in the early 1980s. Inspired by Jean Houston's evocative body of work, including *Life Force*, *The Possible Human*, and *Search for the Beloved*, I recognized the need for attention to women's growth and development issues. Many of my therapy clients became my original "Possible Woman" network.

In workshops held for women by women, we asked those very questions: "Who are you?" and "What could you be?" The search for answers brought many forms of exploration. We offered seminars such as "Women and Sexuality,"

"Lifelong Success for Women," "Interpersonal Communications Training," and "Parent Skills Training for Women." We held other versions of these programs, expanding them to include the outer woman as well as the inner woman. "The Power of the Feminine Spirit," "The Creative Spirit," and "Male-Female, What's the Difference?" were other workshops we created. Through the evolution of these workshops, the vision of the Possible Woman developed, as a seminar and into these writings.

All of these programs were aimed at discovering, for each woman, her strengths, talents, and desires. Many of the participants changed careers and other aspects of their lives as they moved into their true potential. Their follow-up stories illustrate and support the success of the workshops. We often were accused of taking kickbacks from universities since so many of our participants chose to further their education.

Ann (not her real name) was one such woman. Her life had been centered on her husband, her household, and her children. The children were now adults, and Ann was searching for what she wanted to become. The support she gained from the workshop and the women she met there helped her face the changes in her life. She explored her artistic talent and became a good painter. She returned to college, earning a degree in textile design. She now sells her tapestries to commercial establishments, with her artistry expressed in beautiful weavings.

Mary was a woman who came with her two daughters to the workshop. In the safety of the time together, they reached a new level of closeness. All of them spoke of the bond they felt as women.

Julie took the risk of telling one of her darkest secrets in the workshop. She said later that it was like a ten-ton weight coming off her chest and that the secret was not so ominous now that she had shared it in the safety of the circle of women. Two others shared similar stories, so Julie found she was not alone.

A fully awake, aware woman is loaded with possibilities and holds answers to questions not yet conceived. These are the times. Woman is the subject. If you are a woman, I invite you to join in the exciting possibilities. (For men, the possibilities are equally exciting – read on.) The energy of aliveness invites both men and women to join in the journey of the spiral of life, ever transforming the world. The greatest of all transformations is in store with the current rise of the feminine in both genders. Coupled with the possibility of living a full one hundred years or more, there are changes on the horizon that will astound even the most devoted and imaginative reader of science fiction.

The end of the 20th century ushers in a different time and a different age. Women now have more opportunities to join the human race in full partnership. A mere lifetime ago in the United States, my grandmother could not vote, and I could not own property in my own name. Employment opportunities for educated women were limited to teaching, nursing, or secretarial work. Women in managerial positions were rare.

Little by little, piece by piece, things began to change. Sometimes change came first from the legal arena; the Civil Rights Movement removed some job discrimination barriers. Oftentimes customs and attitudes were slower to change, even when legal barriers didn't exist.

In the early 1970s, a recent college graduate who is now a movie producer was asked about her typing skills and told there were "no openings for women" when she applied for work at a television station. During her interview, a male prospective employee who telephoned was invited to apply for floor director, a position on the production crew. When the woman said she was interested in that job, the interviewer said, "Oh, you don't want to do that. It's a man's job, and you'll get dirty." The woman said she didn't mind dirt and continued to press. She was granted an interview for the floor director's job (legally, she couldn't be denied an interview) and was hired after she demonstrated she was able to climb on the lighting grid located fifteen feet above the studio's concrete floor. (She later learned male applicants didn't have to climb on the grid before they were hired.)

Another woman who worked as a secretary for the telephone company realized she could significantly increase her income and work outdoors instead of in an office if she trained to become a lineman, a job previously open only to men. When an opening for a lineman was posted, she applied. Her supervisor discouraged her, but eventually her persistence got her the job.

Today women have more options and more

opportunities to fully contribute. Women's full contribution is a revolutionary concept, for the release of women to full citizenship also releases men to be fully human and fully alive.

The story of woman has many components that are different from the story of man. The most obvious and basic difference is physical. Because her body is equipped to conceive, give birth, and nurse children, her brain has developed to accommodate the necessary complex tasks associated with the nurturing of young. Because of centuries of repression into gender-defined roles, woman has developed with a different brain. Her genetic inheritance, shaped in the crucible of female experience, has given her certain talents. She is able to do many things simultaneously, she tends to many details, and she can manage multiple situations with patience and perseverance. She is the perfect candidate for leadership in the so-called communication age. Corporate America is waking up to the realization that she possesses the skills, endemically, to lead. One of the many qualities woman brings to corporate life is her ability to foster cooperation rather than competition. She is in position to lead, and her talents are exactly right for the job.

Taking charge is not always easy, but it is necessary in order for you to thrive and to make a contribution to the Earth. I encourage all women to claim your past, your story, and your roots. Make your peace with your parents and forgive them. Forgive yourself for choosing them, and get on with writing your own life story. When you do, you will become more awake and aware and interested in yourself and your creation. You are needed. You can flower. You are valued. You can make a very real difference. Believing all this is the first step in your quest to become the Possible Woman. Whoever you are, you are someone I want to know better, and your story is valuable to your world. This book is written to acknowledge you with my hope that you will find inspiration to discover and accept your true potential.

INTRODUCTION

This book is for you.

Maybe you are a woman who climbed the corporate ladder and chose not to marry. Now you find yourself in an executive position, flying everywhere in the company jet, and you tell me that it is like being in a fraternity. The members speak in declarative sentences. They love to compare life to football. Sometimes they forget that your position is equal to theirs. You tell me you sometimes feel invisible.

You may be a man who is sensitive, poetic, in touch with his feelings, and tired of always being expected to be strong. You speak of wanting to "get off the wheel" but because of your obligations, you cannot stop working. You long for time to know your family, to explore your spiritual nature, and find inner peace. You speak about golden handcuffs that keep you tied to your work. You cry and then apologize for your display of emotion. This book is for you. You are a whole human being, and you can find the power of your feminine spirit.

You could be the mother who adopted two children, supported a handicapped husband, and still managed a full time career.

Or maybe you are the mother of four children, one of whom you had when you were only seventeen years old. Your husband has had an affair, and you are devastated.

Are you the one who hides her purchases from her husband or father? You hide them because you care about him. It bothers you to see him so upset over your spending money. So you protect him by lying and hiding your reality.

Perhaps you are a divorced mother and the manager of your own business, married to a man who has children from a former marriage. You have blended your families, and you are confused about the enormity of the demands on you from your business, the children, your husband, and the world around you. (Not to mention fighting a long trip through heavy traffic twice a day only to arrive home, where everyone wants a piece of you just as they did at work all day.) Your stress points are mounting.

Maybe you are the woman who takes care of her aging parents. The woman who is a leader in the world of women's issues. The woman who wishes she could break the bonds of commitment to volunteer services. The woman who wants someone with whom she can share her dreams, hopes, and aspirations.

Perhaps you are the woman who held the family together through addictions, treatment, financial embarrassment, bouts with the legal system, credit card debt, or someone's mental breakdown.

Maybe you are the woman who sought spiritual sustenance and discovered the world of organized religion is still very patriarchal. Maybe you found alternative possibilities for your spiritual devotion, only to be shunned by family and friends.

Are you a woman who is fighting for her life in the throes of a major illness? Your life has been interrupted, and you are making many adjustments and trying to cope.

Just possibly, you are the widow who is 80 years old and whose children are insisting you give up your home when you are not really ready to do so. Or maybe you have become reclusive from most of the world, since you are not really able to trust those who might be advisors.

Perhaps you are a trained, superb artist who is still not paid in keeping with your abilities, education, and/or expertise. (Something is wrong in a world when a medical doctor or lawyer, male or female, is excused for charging high fees on the basis of long education and training. What does this tell us about how our society values art?)

Could you be the woman who finds her mate to be obstinate – even obstructive – when she has a desire, want, need, or feeling? Or maybe the man in your life walked in one day to announce he found someone else or that he "just needs some space."

Maybe you made top grades in school and work for a boss who was a mediocre student but a star athlete. You think faster than he, and you can do many tasks at once. He thinks he's entitled to take credit for your accomplishments, since you work for him.

Do you have secrets that include sexual abuse? Are you one of us who was molested by your father, grandfather, uncle, brother, cousin, neighbor, or minister?

Could you be the woman who knew when she was five years old that she was "different"? Today, you live a semi-secret adult life because you are a lesbian.

Yes, this book is for you.

So you were born female, wrapped in a blanket of pink! How has that affected your life? How has it limited your possibilities? Has it enlarged your possibilities in any way?

Picture this scene. A new baby has been born. An anxious father awaits the news from the birthing room. The grandmother-midwife comes with a crestfallen, apologetic look that announces the sad news: The baby is a girl, but they can try again for a son next year. This story conjures up visions of dark ages, snake pits, witch hunts, and the accumulated helpless rage of an entire gender.

In *The Secret Life of the Unborn Child*, Thomas Verny reports memories of children from the womb. There is clear evidence that we have absorbed details from our in utero experiences: words, ambience, tones of voice, and even the thoughts and feelings of the mother. Babies can be stung and poisoned for life with such birthing room remarks as "I'm sorry, it's a girl! Better luck next time." That little girl inhales an unconscious sense of shame about who she is even as she inhales her first breath. The responses she receives from other relationships reinforce old notions about who girls are or what they should be. The life of any one girl child is responsive to her context. We are each other's context.

My view is that feminine wisdom can usher in a new model, a model not based on woman's becoming anti-male or imitation male with a new conquest-dominance approach. Woman's wisdom, born of repression, is ageless, timeless, and evolutionary. Through the ages, woman survives. She has arrived at the turn of the new century adept, incredibly brilliant, extremely creative, and with a multi-tracking brain-mind system.

I believe that today's Possible Woman wants to express herself emotionally, physically, intellectually, and spiritually. Helping women do that has become my life's mission. Since 1973, I have been a counselor to families, marriages, and individuals. In that work, I am a change agent in the lives of women. My hope for each individual female is that she finds a path of contribution, crafted in her personal, unique brilliance, that becomes her story. My goal is to provide the teaching and mentoring that ease and encourage her to own and develop her story. I call it joining the "Triple A." The challenge-opportunity is to become the Author, Actor, and Audience in one's own life story.

WHO IS THE POSSIBLE WOMAN?

The Possible Woman is a new model. She is a healthy, whole, female person with a positive, internal sense of self, capable of many expressions of her talents. Her talents are defined as her aptitudes, capacities, and abilities. When her talents are given expression, she brings her unique contribution to the world through achievements based in her original design.

The Possible Woman arrives in the world with the human capabilities for love, joy, peace, and altruism. She can learn, she can work, she can play, and she can love. She is not limited because of her gender. All human beings, regardless of gender, have original vision, incredible determination, and talents to be developed. Through the millennia of time, woman has been shaped in the crucible of the ages to be cooperative, collaborative, and more interested in process than product. The Possible Woman is, in her very nature, life giving, life honoring, life nurturing, and life sustaining.

The vital life force directing the growth of any human embryo is like the potential blossoming of a plant to fullest flower. The purpose of the life force of an acorn is to become a giant oak tree. As it does, the acorn is "actualized" – its very essence comes forth in actual form. The purpose of the life force of a human infant is to become an unfolded, blossoming "godling" who will benefit the human race. The potential of the Possible Woman is to become actualized in reality, not to be less than herself, perfect and beautiful. To become all she can be requires the cumulative effect of her development throughout her stages of capacities and abilities. These capabilities are her talents, and the Possible Woman passionately yearns to express them.

This Possible Woman I envision is a collective organism, born of the angst of centuries, skilled at the tasks necessary for future generations, and, with an updated self-concept, free to become all she can become. She is ready to blossom. Her essential self is unfolding. Her potential is in motion.

Women can speak, write, and express in ways that are new to the world. The power of the feminine spirit holds the power to bring life, to nurture life, to bring hope, to foster peace, to arbitrate, to negotiate, and to love. Woman has been the backbone of the family, and she knows how to nurture, in a positive way, a family or other group of human beings.

Throughout this book, I will speak of the essence of you as an individual. You are a seed with great potential. Your true self is waiting to be nurtured into existence. The seed of your true self is the essence of your individual being – a beautiful seed filled with enormous potential.

THE POSSIBLE WOMAN BOOK

Please join me for seven chapters of reading and transformational exercises in pursuit of the development of the Possible Woman.

The first three chapters remember the past and ask, "Who are we?" Chapter 1 recalls the broad time divisions of woman's roots as she developed through the "Ages." In Chapter 2, we review the confinement of woman in cultural "Cages" – the things that keep us from becoming Possible Women. Chapter 3 provides a transforming focus for women who are caught in "Rages."

The middle chapters ask, "How can we grow

and change?" In Chapter 4, "Pages," the value of woman's traits in the communication-information age is discussed with the necessity for the joys of lifelong learning. Chapter 5 identifies one individual's life "Stages" with an emphasis on women's relational talents.

The last two chapters address the question, "What could we be?" Chapter 6 is about parity and equity in modern day and future "Wages." Chapter 7, "Sages," is about the timeless and ageless wisdom of women.

In each chapter, you'll find exercises noted by the symbol of a leaf. These exercises will help you, the reader, "turn over a new leaf." They are helpful in your most important life task, which is to answer the questions, "Who am I?" and "What can I become?"

In the Appendix A in the back of the book, you'll find a description of the Possible Woman Workshop I devised and conducted. Please feel free to use it as a guide to create your own workshop or weekend retreat.

In Appendix B, you'll find a list of recommended readings that includes titles I have found useful and helpful.

CHAPTER ONE

AGES

*Every woman's story is built
on the stories of all the women
who have ever lived.*

Universal patterns – archetypes – exist in the collective whole of all women. Each individual woman lives a life that reflects archetypal patterns. Like computer generated fractal pictures, there is a general sameness with each pattern, even though each new occurrence seems different. I have lived this life for seven decades, and I have discovered that all the things that happen to me, good or bad, happen in patterns, and I am the only one consistently present. Some of these patterns are unique to me because I am female. Mothering, wifing, and daughtering are female fractal waves with some commonalties for all females. The archetype called "mother" is universal. So is "mate." The female as daughter to her mother is a pattern we hold in common with all females.

Information
Mechanic

Factory Worker

Farmer~Protector

Hunter

Life Force Taproot

The tribe or family of origin into which we were born as females influenced the beginnings of our personal patterns. These patterns create our story, which shapes and reveals our character. Many emotional events from our childhood leave an impact on us. These remain part of our "oddities," our unique character, our different personality. They are chapters in our ongoing life story.

I am amazed at the many lifetimes I have lived since my birth in 1929. I knew a world limited to one farm

Gifts from the Past

Information
Intuitive

Who are you?
What could you be?

Hearth Keeper

Gardener-Nurturer

Gatherer

community without modern conveniences. My father farmed with horses. We had no telephone, television, radio, or electricity. We milked cows by hand, hauled our water from the windmill that drew from a well drilled deeply into the earth. We had kerosene lamps to light our nighttime, slept on feather beds, and learned to cook, sew, and work the farm. We called the entire family to rush outside and see an airplane high in the sky, for it was a miraculous happening. When we got a windcharger and had our first low wattage, pull-chain, single-bulb-in-the-ceiling electric lights, we were wide-eyed with the wonders of modern civilization.

I remember being fascinated by the life around me and delighting in the joy of learning. Whether it was learning to read, to add and subtract, or to help with quilting, gardening, or feeding the hogs, I eagerly reached for new possibilities.

In another life, I was a traditional wife and stay-at-home mother. In the post World War II era, I married a returning veteran, gave birth to his four children, and helped him further his education. He died four years after receiving his doctorate in theoretical physics and I was appalled that "our" degree died with him. My children were virtually orphaned as I faced life alone, a single parent without the means to support them.

Other lives I have lived as a schoolteacher, a counselor, and a graduate student earning my own doctorate. I could not conceive of the enormity of change that would take place in technology, science, and industry. To imagine a talking picture show (in color) in our own living room was impossible. To comprehend e-mail and the Internet was unthinkable. Computers were not even in the vocabulary. I now understand that my dreams were too small because I could not conceive of the burst of possibilities soon to be available to us. In truth, I have met all the goals I set in childhood and have far exceeded my limited expectations. The pattern consistent through it all was my fascination with learning. I could not stretch beyond the limits of my experience. The women around me also seemed held in by cultural limitations. They didn't question their rights or talk about equality. Those ideas were not yet on the horizon.

What I have learned from many great teachers and mentors is that our mind-brain-body systems are capable of far more than we have yet imagined. We can, through the process of our own differentiation, reach for a better, more peaceful, more fulfilled existence as women.

I invite you to remember your grandmothers. Look backward into your story as girls, wives, mothers, aunts, grandmothers, single women, nieces, and all your female forbears. They hold the patterns of your existence, your development, and your life as a woman. We have commonalties that are strong and that impact our existence, yet we are often almost unaware of them or take them for granted.

All women have a common pool of experience. From the beginning of time, we have come as a gender through certain ages with a female-specific set of talents and skills, developed because we have the body of the female of the human species. Ownership of ovaries, uterus, vagina, mammary glands, and the hormones these body parts require is a common pattern for every female.

GATHERERS-SHOPPERS

Women were gatherers in long-ago tribes of hunter-gatherer nomads. As gatherers, we developed a sharp eye for detail, and the ability to spot the best foodstuffs is encoded in our very DNA. As modern world citizens, women possess the native talents of born shoppers. We go to a store and select the best, just as our grandmothers of old could gather the prize roots, nuts, and berries. We take our time, often enjoying the gathering process as much as the purchase itself. Retailers today understand that it's good business to accommodate the female urge to forage and gather, so they display their goods on easily accessed, attractive counters that encourage browsing and make the shopping experience more interesting and fun. Some researchers estimate that the female gatherer was responsible for 80% of the food while the male hunter brought home only 20%. Today, women spend about 80% of the family income.

My favorite yarn illustrating the hunter-gatherer heritage starts with the hunt. The whole tribe, clad in animal skin clothing, is chasing a wooly mammoth. The warrior males spear the animal. Afterwards, waiting for the slab of fresh meat to cook, the men sit around talking about the great hunt and exciting kill. The women, in the meantime, gut the mammoth, skin it, cut up the meat, and drag it back to camp where they will make jerky, tan the hide for clothing, and bear babies on the way. The men, having made the kill, are finished. The women are multi-trackers. They think of every-thing, they do everything. They are us. We can be impatient with anyone who gets in our way.

Physically, we have developed in accord with our hunter-gatherer past. Even the rods and cones in our eyes reflect this difference. Men have a keener use of the cones, the tissue in our seeing apparatus that allows us to focus on one thing, narrowing the range of vision. Females have more rod-centered vision (rods enable us to see a wide range of visual stimuli) and have more advanced peripheral vision. The old idea that "Mama has eyes in the back of her head" is not too far from the physical truth.

Today we reap the harvest of these millennia of thought processes. Some of our thought patterns include compartmentalized beliefs: men are strong, and women are weak; men are objective, women are subjective; men are level-headed, women are emotional. A more accurate view is that women endure because they are familiar with emotions and are not scared to experience and express their feel-ings. Woman's multi-tracking talent includes her awareness and alertness to the emotional flow of a family. Mothers read the moods of family members. The warrior-hunter male "guts up and goes on." The hidden messages of the hunter are that big boys don't cry, and emotions can be denied without consequences. Girls are soft and allowed to cry, even expected to cry, because they are weak. But women can exhibit strength, and men can exhibit weakness. And sometimes there is strength in weakness (it may be better not to resist the mugger who wants your wallet); sometimes there is weakness in strength (trying to tough it out all the time can be a recipe for a heart attack).

In Rob Becker's one man show, *Defending the Cave Man*, he says in one scene that when his wife asked him to share his feelings, Rob replied, "I feel like I want to watch TV!" The remote control is a great new weapon. He takes aim at the channels while she dusts, makes beds, peels potatoes, crochets, feeds babies, and reads. Her brain multi-tracks, accessing many things at once. He's watching television, unaware of his surroundings.

Mary was a client who came to me to work on her frustration about her husband's lack of interest in her and her life. Her desire was to have a closer relationship. Mary told me a scheme she used to get her husband's attention. She would stand in front of the TV until he realized his picture was blocked. Then he would ask her what she wanted, and she could have a brief conversation.

When her husband came to a therapy session, she told him she wanted more time to talk with him in private with no television or distraction. He wanted to know why. She spoke of her desire to have a more intimate relationship, rekindling their love passion and exploring their feelings. He seemed mystified but, dutifully, said he would try to change. Mary said she felt he was insincere. Both of them warmed to the idea that they were different in temperament. Basically, he personified maleness, and she typified femaleness. Eventually, they were able to lighten up and be amused by their differences. The conversations they had following their laughter enabled them to make conscious changes. Now she can ask for his attention, and he gives it if he can. She is more tolerant of his need to focus on television programs such as ball games and golf matches.

This old male-female scene is stereotypical. Men as single-focused hunters, women as multi-tracking gatherers is a remnant of history, and some men and some women still exemplify these stereotypes. Today, though remnants of the gatherer-hunter age still exist, we have the promise of becoming whole as individuals without strict, separate definitions based on gender. There are new possibilities for both males and females. We are just beginning to realize we can accept and express all of our functions – feeling, thinking, sensing, and acting – and take responsibility for them.

Masculine and feminine are not concrete and absolute descriptors of any man or woman. Individual men can develop and express a feminine side, and individual women can find interior masculinity. A whole person is one who accepts the presence of both masculine and feminine.

Think about how your perception of words influences how you perceive others and yourself. Here are some examples: Words such as "rational," "focused," "objective," and "detached" are often used to describe male behavior and generally are considered positive. Words such as "irrational," "scattered," "subjective," and "emotional" are often used to decribe female behavior and generally are considered negative. Why? Think of times when it is not necessary or beneficial to be rational or focused, objective or detached. And when might it be appropriate and good to be irrational or scattered, subjective or emotional? Listen to what you say, and hear others as they talk.

FARMERS-PRODUCERS

The next age came when some gatherers took a stick, poked a hole in the ground, and planted a few seeds to germinate after the tribe wandered to the next place to seek another wooly mammoth. When the tribe returned the next season, a crop was growing. In this new agrarian age, instead of following the food, people settled down in one place, planted, cultivated, and harvested food, and domesticated animals. Tribal families chose a plot of ground for growing crops, and they established territoriality. As females, we needed a protector so we found a husband, and he got a wife. We built a house, established a nest to raise our children and hold our possessions, and began protecting the territory and all the stuff. We began to accumulate. Competition came on the scene. Competition for ownership and territory, comparison to our neighbor, and the necessity of having enough food and clothing to last until the next harvest brought about rivalry. (I'm speaking in generalities, of course. Not all of our ancestors fought each other, and some cultures even today cannot understand nor do they accept our need to fence things in and own them.) Wars became the *modus operandi* for the holding of ownership. Marriage became the legal status for ownership of mates.

In the serfdoms, kingdoms, and farms of the agrarian age, women had a very real place. A husband and a wife, a king and a queen, a father and a mother were helpmates. They worked as a team. Each had a job to do, and each was important. Men and women had distinct and separate roles. Neither was to assume the role of the other; to do so was to betray the species. Men were men, and women were women. Women married, had children, and did "women's work," the tasks of presiding over the household. Men protected the territory while they tilled the soil and planted and harvested crops. Family roles were distinct and unbending. The "ideal" of the self-sufficient nuclear family, with a strong father and a stay-at-home mother, remains as a vestige of this age of ownership and territoriality.

In the agrarian age, men and women worked

very hard, tilling the soil, growing crops, tending animals, and making their household necessities like soap, candles, and cloth. Women had as many babies as they could because the family needed help with the farming. The conscious awareness of feelings, other than physical ones, was not emphasized. Women worked from dawn to dusk to survive, and often died before they could speak about emotions, feelings, or other awarenesses of our modern age. Many women didn't live past menopause, so they didn't need to think of life beyond daughtering, wifing, and mothering. Most men didn't live to be old, so they didn't have to worry about mid-life crises. Death was the culmination of many people's mid-life crisis.

Hard physical labor or the management of slaves or serfs kept the kingdom – or the farm – thriving. Disease, hunger, and war were the norms for life in the agrarian age. The evolutionary thrust was to become more efficient: to mechanize the operation, to make superior weapons to protect the land and to make better tools to make it easier to tend the animals, till the soil, and harvest the crops. The development of farming tools was the beginning of a period of technical and industrial expansion.

INDUSTRIAL/TECHNICAL/MECHANICAL

With tools, we progressed to the technical-industrial age. Factories, machinery, and mechanization coincided with Newtonian physics and Skinnerian psychology. In the age of technical expansion, such simple, predictable explanations were ideal. (While Newton's and Skinner's theories were necessary steps in the continuum of our intellectual growth, we are now at a different place on the continuum.)

Newton saw an apple fall from a tree and gave us a new way to see the physical world. Cause-effect thinking became the exciting new science. Newton presumed the act of observance was objective and benign. Quantum theory, developed in the middle of the 20th century, says the very act of observing is dynamic and creative and that observing affects both the observer and the observed.

Skinner's theories of human behavior also followed a cause-effect theme. Behavioral management became a mechanistic act of applying or withholding a reinforcer. In experiments, the chicken rang the bell for food because a food pellet appeared when the bell rang. Extrapolated to childrearing, Skinner's theories held that children will behave according to the focus of parental attention – what is attended to gets repeated, and the operator (the parent) is assumed to be benign and objective. Modern relationship theory contends context influences behavior.

In 20th century America, women had received the right to vote, and some autonomy was offered to females. Many women established themselves as the wife who stayed at home and supported the husband who manned the factory.

We helped in war efforts throughout the ages by nursing, holding the home front, tending the children, teaching in the schools, and volunteering in the churches. World War II brought possibilities for women as WACS and WAVES and in defense plants. The men were drafted into the military, and the factories needed womanpower. Rosie the Riveter was a war hero, her hair in a snood, smiling and wearing trousers.

Rosie was handed a pink slip the day after the war ended in 1945, and though she was told to allow the men to be the breadwinners while she was the homemaker, she was searching for a self that wanted expression. That self started to show up. Small numbers of women began to change tradition quietly but dramatically. More women entered medical school, and others became engineers and scientists. Using her female capability of multi-tracking, some Rosies kept the factory job and the household management job, becoming two-shift workers. The first shift covered the eight hours spent at the factory-office-institution (paid); the other shift began when the woman arrived home and began the household management (unpaid) tasks. The two-shift worker can resent a spouse who only works one (paid) shift.

In my therapy practice, a woman client often brings in her husband to "get him fixed" – she doesn't think he helps enough around the house. As I work with them, we negotiate his beginning to share the load, and a new dimension of their relationship develops. I ask, who decorates your home? Who sets the schedule for your family? Who decides how you spend your money? In the majority of cases, she does.

A woman who is pursuing her potential may not realize that her mate is still learning to be equal partner and needs the opportunity to gracefully share the full load. Often she sees herself as the owner of the cave – their home. When he begins to do laundry, cook, clean, and tend the babies, she may criticize him and want him to do it her way. She may need to assess how much she remains mired in the old traditional roles because she believes her husband incapable of the tasks and how attached she is to maintaining an autocratic, top-down, controlling management style in their home.

My husband Paul and I often share and reverse roles at home. Perhaps because I was first born, I learned "masculine" activities, such as driving the tractor; perhaps because he was second born (and his mother intended that he be a girl), Paul learned to babysit and became a very good cook. A friend stopped by our home recently and found Paul in the kitchen cooking dinner. I was upstairs changing out a doorknob. Our friend called us weird. We don't think we are.

THE AGE OF INFORMATION

From nomadic wanderers with our training as gatherers to farm wives who could spin and make soap to the modern Millies of the office and factory, we have arrived at the beginning of the next era. The 21st century ushers in a new age, the age of

information and communication, an age of partic-
ipatory management at home and in the workplace.

The so-called communication age is a natural
for woman, thanks to her experience with multi-
tasking. Woman is equipped to communicate feelings, thoughts, opinions, facts, and beliefs.
Estimates are that a woman needs to say seven
thousand words per day versus a man's two thousand per day. When they meet after work, he may
have exhausted his supply of words for the day, but
she still may have more than a thousand words she
needs to speak. To keep peace, she shuts down,
swallows her words, or finds another means of
expression.

The female brain is uniquely ready for this age
of information and communication. As a secretary,
wife, teacher, or nurse, or in another supporting
role, she has become an expert in the areas of
details and information. She knows the intricacies
of the office and the home. Sometimes, the scene is
one where he tries to find his socks, and she knows
where they are; he wants the insurance policy, and
she knows where it is; her boss needs a phone number, and she knows where to find it. She is a vast

reservoir of information. Her intuition is available at all times. She intuits that a child or a pet or a plant is in trouble before it happens. She can guess her husband's mood from the sound of his footsteps as he enters the house. She often worries before the fact and can make predictions with astounding accuracy. Her brain seems to be equipped to access both right and left sides instantly. Her corpus callosum, the connective tissue between the right and left sides of the neocortex, is physically larger than a man's, having spent eons processing a multitude of tasks and details. Her brain is configured to multi-track and multi-task. She can do many things at once. Because her body is configured to conceive, give birth, and nurture, she has become accustomed through the ages to offer nurturing and caring. Her heart energy knows the bond with all other hearts. In essence, she is very smart.

Ashley Montague's book of anthropological facts, *The Natural Superiority of Women*, first published in 1952, describes the ways in which women handle stress, physical illness, and daily life with more stamina and determination than men. Montague points out the physical fact that women live longer. He considered them "inferior" in only one category: most do not possess the physical prowess of males.

Most modern jobs, however, don't require physical prowess or strength. As women gain entry to the entire spectrum of employment and the full range of stressful endeavors, we are discovering men and women may be more alike than Montague thought. Women now succumb to stress-related illnesses in the same percentages as men when they enter formerly male-only or male-dominated professions and careers. But even though women now suffer more heart attacks and contract more lung cancer than they once did, many other feminine strengths have been built through the passages of the past.

The Possible Woman is ready to enter the 21st century with all the talents, skills, and genius born of a long history as a second class citizen of her world. Her minority status is shifting to full partnership. We, women and men, are rapidly preparing to work together for the healing of the Earth.

We can live in a more hopeful communion with all life. Protection and competition are the roots of war. We learned how to fear one another, make one another the enemy, and fight in increasingly sophisticated ways. Cooperation and helpful caring as we knew it in the caves faded into suspicion, jealousy, and fear.

We reached the apex of these patterns of competitive dominance-conquest when we achieved the capability of destroying the known world. More recent events – the fall of the Berlin Wall, the end of the Cold War, and the arrival of instant global communication – bring hope for a better tomorrow. Communication and information sharing include the opening of knowledge from East to West. When religious separatism fades, wisdom of other cultures is available. The picture of our world, as viewed from outer space for the first time in this century, is that of one small orb. The planet Earth appears as a gray-green-blue marble suspended against the black velvet of space. We are tiny creatures in a vast macrocosm of the universe. We are connected, and we are one Earth tribe.

We will learn that the enemy is the same as us, if not really us. We can return to a balance of words and images. We can stretch our capacity toward the frontal lobes of our incredible brains to the path of altruism, opening to heart wisdom, and making it safe for one another.

Our confining roles as the warrior male and the childbearing female are now outmoded. With six billion humans living on this small, beautiful planet, we can limit our warfare and our childbearing. We must learn to live together in harmony with animals, plants, humans, and all of life. Sustaining all life on Earth becomes the new endeavor for us.

Walk backward through the generations of women who were your mothers and grandmothers. Imagine the life of each of your female progenitors. Think of the world your mother inhabited when she was pregnant with you: her worries, her fears, her joys, and her learning. Do the same for both grandmothers, all four great-grandmothers, and eight great-great grandmothers. Imagine their lives. Project yourself into the body of each. Try to imagine the experience of being her for a period of time. Talk with a helpful friend, or journal what you discover. Then return to the age of the nomadic wanderer, and imagine being one of those grandmothers. Report or record what you imagine.

We are living in a possibility time. Woman, for the first time in recorded history, is included. We should no longer apologize for our brilliance or our industry.

As we approach the 21st century, we are ready for the contribution of woman. As one single, individual woman, your story is an important contribution for the whole of humankind. Believing that, thinking that, and knowing that is the task of the Possible Woman.

CHAPTER TWO

CAGES

- *What limits you?*
- *What holds you back from your greatest potential?*
- *What binds you?*

As a small girl child in the first half of the 20th century, it never occurred to me that I was growing up with a limited number of possibilities. My horizons were limited by the cage of my gender. I could be a daughter, a wife, a mother, and possibly a school-teacher like my mother had been. I also could serve my world through the church by being a musician, which meant being a choir member, a pianist, or organist. I did not consciously have ambitions beyond that. To become a choir director, a school superintendent, a minister, or a county judge were not possibilities I consciously perceived.

Just as fish do not discover water because it is all around them, I was not awake to gender-based constraints. Those boundaries were a cage of

Gender–Based Limits

Born
Female

Different
Body

Different
Brain

Religion

Cultural
Constraints

Survival
Adaptations

44

confinement, a container beyond which I could not grow. I could not see what I did not know. The seed of my life, my essential self, could grow only so far and no farther. I was unaware, and unconscious. I was contained in body, mind, and spirit because I was born a girl.

A DIFFERENT BODY

The difference between my male counterparts and me was the male/female separation – the split based on gender. It was a cage built on physical characteristics that I had no power to control. Why did I not think of myself as a potential corporation CEO, a preacher who led a congregation, a school superintendent who built a better education system, a land owner, or a political leader who made a difference in the world of government? Why did I deny myself such possibilities? I could read, write, spell, and do arithmetic better than most of the boys in my school. I could do most of the chores on the farm.

My body was female, and I was

taught to expect happiness through romantic love. There was a popular song from the Roaring 20s, "She's Only a Bird in a Gilded Cage." The bird in the cage sings, and so did young women in my era. Romantic songs about yearnings and longings spoke to dreams of comfort and love. "Somewhere, Over the Rainbow" and "Someday, My Prince Will Come" were examples of the caged bird singing of her hopes for the good life. I was among those women who went to college, studied for a degree, and planned for a career as a sort of life insurance policy, but my true ambition was to date a lot of men, find the right one, marry, establish my home, and rear my children. I was unaware that my dream depended on finding a man who would furnish the financial wherewithal for this to happen. This was the way it was supposed to be. It was as if I were a Japanese bonsai – a lovely work of art, but severely pruned and shaped by outside forces.

Shaping and pruning according to birth identity were still practiced in the world. Slavery had been abolished and suffrage had been legalized, but the era of my youth was still one in which roles were assigned because of being born male or female. At very subtle levels of interaction, I was not permitted the fullest flower of my potential growth, but I cooperated because I wanted to survive and desired to belong.

I had more questions than answers, many questions that went unasked: Was I destined to live as a dependent daughter, wife, and mother? If that was my destiny, how would I cope with the truth that our Earth has become overpopulated? Did I really need to dedicate my life to the principal tasks of bearing children, nursing children, and tending a home? Was I more than a nurturer to my family? Would I have a life outside their needs? How would I function when my children were out of the nest and on their own? Since I didn't need to bring more children into the world, how could I best serve the world, realizing I could live one hundred years or more?

A DIFFERENT BRAIN

To answer some of my questions, I looked at my life. I examined my beliefs, my attitudes, my values, and especially those concepts that were based only on gender. This led me to the study of how we think, how we make choices, and what makes us act the way we do, feel the way we feel, and keep believing old notions that may be outmoded.

I learned about our brains. One idea I read was that female brains have developed to reflect the qualities attached to nurturing. Tending to children and the complexities of hearth and home management requires agile, quick thinking. Decisions must be made in a split second and are often of life or death importance. The corpus callosum has more neuronal connections in female brains. Common belief holds that this is a necessary brain development, based on the female's need to access both halves of the brain rapidly. Since the female must tend to multiple caretaking tasks and all the organization needed to multi-track them, her brain has developed accordingly.

From the work of Dr. Paul MacLean at the National Institutes of Health, I learned the triune brain model and found it very useful as a metaphor for understanding human foibles. MacLean said we have an old survival brain that physically corresponds to the brains of reptiles. The reptilian complex he described is located in a ganglion of cells resting at the top of the spinal column near the base of the brain. Similar to reptiles, we humans are creatures of habit, cold-blooded, seeking above all to survive. MacLean described the second part of the brain, which is the limbic system, as the first mammalian brain. Warm-blooded and nurturing, this part of the brain directs the hormonal flow of humans and other mammals. The third and largest part of the brain is the neocortex. It contains our problem-solving ability, our creative imagination, our technical prowess, and our ability to think. The right and left halves of the neocortex form our thinking brain, which allows us to make words and pictures.

Dr. MacLean and other researchers speak also of the frontal lobes. This most recent part of the brain, which rests in the foreheads of modern *homo sapiens*, was less developed in Neanderthal and Cro-Magnon humans. Present-day scientists conjecture that this frontal lobe might be the seat of empathy and altruism. Research is still revealing the function of this fourth part of the brain.

Harville Hendrix utilizes the triune brain model in his book, *Getting the Love You Want: A Guide for Couples*. Hendrix's Imago Relationship Theory is a model I embraced and continue to use effectively in my work with relationships. Imago theory helps us learn new ways of being as individuals, better ways of communing with others, advanced ways of relating, and concepts that help us create a vision for a future of loving relationships. It provides a practical process whereby we can break the cages of our limitations and mature beyond our childhood woundings. Through loving relationships, we are released from the confinement based on gender. In the crucible of relationships, we can recover our unique spirit as individuals.

RELIGION

The religions of my culture also provided a bar, reinforced by fearful images, to the cage of being female. Male leaders spoke as representatives of the powerful male god and I, a female, received the "truth" that my place was divined and defined according to male interpretations. Why did I not ask questions? There was an underlying pool of fear that at best I would be ridiculed; at worst, those I loved most would reject me. So I held my tongue and gained my power within the limits of what was available to women of my era.

My curiosity led me to readings in anthropology and archeology that revealed human beings once worshipped both gods and goddesses – deities both male and female, portrayed in many forms. There is evidence of well-formed and culturally dominant goddess religions in Europe, where high priestesses in long robes were the spiritual leaders. (Today, when I see male clergy in their long robes, I wonder where that idea originated.) These ancient religions celebrated the harvest and the bounty of the Earth with rituals and ceremonies designed by women. But the goddess religions died out. What happened? Why and when did God become a man?

A fascinating theory is posited by Leonard Shlain in his book, *The Alphabet Versus the Goddess*. Shlain makes a plausible argument that something significant brought about centuries of male conquest and dominance and the masculine form of God we now worship. He suggests that significant something was literacy! The advent of the alphabet, he proposes, spelled the demise of the goddess as leader in the world of the spiritual life and cultural beliefs by fostering left brain development at the expense of right brain development. His argument makes great sense, since reading – perceiving words on a page in sequence – is a function of the "masculine" left brain.

Shlain further suggests that the teachings of Jesus of Nazareth, with their attention to empathy, understanding, and love, moved us toward "feminine" right brain emotionality and imagery. Jesus taught through pictures, parables, and stories, and he didn't write anything down. He devalued strict adherence to law and judgment and spoke of two commandments, the first about loving God and the second about loving your neighbor as yourself. Jesus also declared there was neither male nor female. Our concept of this equality and the Christ love that surpasses understanding have yet to find a place in our world. In a speech, I once spoke about God in feminine form and subsequently received hate mail (from women!), so I chose the less courageous path of becoming invisible and holding my thoughts to myself.

CULTURE

Every little girl's first seven years require cooperation with the messages from the elders. In return for her cooperation, the elders feed, clothe, and shelter her. Unfortunately, these become habits of dependence that are deeply ingrained. Young elephants chained to a strong, immovable steel stake grow to be adults conditioned to stand prisoner to a chain around one leg that is tied to a simple short wooden stick. The adult elephant could easily walk away, but its brain has the memory of the cage, and long after the real imprisonment is ended, the limit is still honored. So it is with many individual women who remain convinced they are victims of the world they inhabit.

One woman, Sara, who was distressed over her life and wanted to break free of her depressing, boring existence told me all the reasons why she could not move to another city, even though she wanted to very badly. She imagined that she could not find a job, and she talked at length about how her mother didn't want her to move. She needed to work for money, and she needed her mother's approval. Overcoming her fears about loss of financial and emotional support was a process of waking up, growing up, and becoming truly conscious about her intentions and her responsibilities. Sara moved the next year and found a better job, Her mother adjusted to the new care situation Sara arranged for her. Sara now is surprised at how she felt so trapped by the fears. Her new job was not that hard to find, and her mother actually expressed relief that Sara had "moved on."

I remember another woman who heard me speak at a conference. She came to me with the words, "I want to be just like you!" I thanked her for the compliment and answered some of her questions. She asked how I had combined my life as a wife and mother with a full time career. I told her my story, revealing the fears I faced when I went back to school. I was in classes with much younger, more adept students; I still felt the responsibility for my home and family. I spoke to her about how I worked with my anxiety through therapy, which included self-hypnosis. I remembered that Carl Jung, the great psychologist who revered God, said that all psychotherapy is spiritual. It is related to beliefs and internal flow. I assured her that our inner work is never-ending. Self-talk, affirmations, and responsible action based on awareness coupled with lightening up on guilt, shame, and fear are necessary ingredients in the creation of possibilities for women. I wanted her to know how self-direction comes from the inside, not necessarily from someone giving encouragement or permission from the outside.

The same woman called me recently. She started

a new business of her own following her graduation. Her enthusiasm was impressive. She expressed how she felt she was really in charge of her life. She engages in meditation and affirmation of herself daily. Her husband and children are proud of her and, contrary to her fears, she is in a new spiral of growth that didn't destroy her happy life. In contrast to her former fears, her fulfillment and expansion into her true potential have enhanced her family life. She reported her husband's new interest in gourmet cooking and his increasing involvement in the lives of their children.

SURVIVAL

Why does woman stay caged? First, she does it to survive. Her old brain (the reptilian and limbic systems) is geared to fight, flee, freeze, or fix the problem. These F-words keep her in the cage of fear. If she is safe, she is able to experience the "good Fs" of fun, food, and frolic and enter into the flow of her life, embracing her freedom. But woman is not always safe. Survival must be her first consideration, and she will tend to respond from fear.

If a woman feels unworthy or if her feelings, desires, or ambitions are judged inappropriate, her self-concept suffers and she will adapt to survive. Stereotypically, we have been assessed as insane when our feelings are out of control. Many times, that diagnosis came from the men in our lives. In the history of the field of mental illness, most of the doctors were male and most of the patients were female.

We have blamed our menses, our PMS, our menopause, and many other "female" problems for our emotional mood swings. We have taken all kinds of medicine to deny the natural flow of our feelings and aid us in conforming to expected cultural standards. One old "scientific" theory identified the "wandering uterus" as the culprit. As if the variety of moods spelled some sort of maladaption, we continued to hold the old beliefs that the female was just an emotion-filled object with potential for breakdown. The word "hysteria," hardly a positive descriptor, is derived from the Greek word *hystero*, which means "uterus."

Our history includes many harsh, inhumane eras, including times when women were tried and convicted as witches. Carol F. Karlsen researched state records and discovered that the majority of women convicted as witches in the Salem witch trials were in line to inherit property because they had no brothers or sons. Others were midwives and healers at a time when medical doctoring was becoming a male profession. Karlsen recounts her research in her book, *The Devil in the Shape of a Woman*. The memory of that persecution rests in women's genetic collective memory. Out of fear, a woman of my era didn't question the cultural mores any more than women in oppressive societies today do not question authority for fear of torture or death. The early programming has worked very well.

FAMILY

In my childhood, each family served the good of the village and its culture, through birth, marriage, all of life, and death.

We didn't question the importance of keeping the family intact. My father and grandfathers were kind and caring men. They protected and looked after their families with integrity and loyalty. They were dedicated servant leaders, giving no time to self-pity or complaints about their lot in life. They respected and cared for their aging relatives, adored babies, and cherished their children, female and male. Widows and orphans were among their responsibilities. Their strengths and their example are a part of my psyche.

Today's culture seems to send the message that the family exists for a different purpose, to serve the individual. If family, spouse, or parent does not meet the desires of the individual, the culture supports abandoning the family. Children blame their parents for their problems, and marriage is conditional. Our so-called "divorce culture" characterizes the individual as one who believes we no longer are bound in committed relationships by internal loyalty to marriage, home, family, and community.

Debate over what caused the change is widespread. Emotionally charged opinions range from blaming and complaining to explaining. Whatever the cause, we can observe the effect on this culture. A cage based on the reality of physical limits also supplied well-defined, secure roles for men and women. When the culture seems to de-emphasize anything except role-confining definitions, a great clash ensues. Individual rights conflict with the survival of the family.

Women seeking equality have not destroyed the nuclear family of my childhood. Farm life and the hard labor it demanded were great equalizers.

Everyone's work was needed to make the family's livelihood. Necessities for the family included more than money, shelter, and food. Emotional flow, tender loving care, physical touch, and attention to each individual family member are all necessities for strong family life. In my farm community these were assumed. As we entered the technical-industrial age, things began to change.

Since World War II, women have been a vital part of the work force, and it's estimated that more than half the work force in 2000 will be female. When my generation of women went to work, we kept the roles of wife and mother. In effect, we developed full left brain capacities for reasoning and logic without inviting males to develop the right brain characteristics of loving, caring, and creativity. We continued to "own the cave," thus staying in the cage. To leave the cage, women have to surrender partial ownership of the cave.

Post-technical era women are asking for partnership in the family. Women have assumed responsibility for providing their share of financial support, thereby inviting men to assume their share of responsibility for nurturing the individual members of the family. A family is a system made up of a collection of individuals. Each individual is affected by and, more importantly, affects the whole unit. The family as a social unit is much too fragile to survive without full cultural dedication to enhancing it.

In non-Western cultures, the picture of contented people who didn't follow the pathway of romantic love but were married to someone chosen by parents or others in an arranged marriage may be a model we admire, for they have families that endure. But that model remains blind to advancing evolutionary changes in the role definitions imposed on males and females. The image of each performing according to cultural tradition denies the truth of individual differences and individual freedom.

That expression "family values" is today's code word for the old nuclear family of the post-World War II economic boom, best exemplified by the television programs of the era, such as *The Adventures of Ozzie and Harriet* and *Father Knows Best*. In those families, where Dad worked in an office and wore a tie, Mom stayed home in a dress and an apron, and the children went to school and played with other kids in the neighborhood, roles were strictly defined and predictable. (And the real men, women, *and children* who portrayed these happy-go-lucky suburbanites were, in fact, *working*.) The fictitious family life portrayed on early television shows has had tremendous staying power precisely because it was captured on film for broadcast. The 1999 movie, *Pleasantville*, was a parody of those naive years and showed the contrast between then and now. The 1950s television images have persisted long after the era they were intended to portray. A call to return to those days of "family values" isn't grounded in reality and does not address the true needs of the single parent, individuality, the female parity issue, and the rights of males to be in full partnership in the nurturing of children.

Women can preach, women can teach, women can heal, women can theorize, women can philosophize, women can build, women can fight, women can do all the things that have been kept from them because of their gender cage. It's just as important to acknowledge the concept that men can nurture, men can express emotions, and men can intuitively solve problems. Men and women need encouragement for balancing their right and left brain abilities. When we reach a balance of equal value for masculine and feminine qualities, we create the possibility of reaching peace and prosperity on planet Earth.

If you are female, make a list of all the ways you have been affected by your gender. Complete the sentences, "Because I was born female, I must..." and "If I had been born male, I could...." If you are male, complete the sentences, "Because I was born male, I must..." and "If I had been born female, I could...." Summarize, either in writing or by talking with a group of friends, the list of life influences you have experienced because of your gender.

OUT OF THE CAGE

How do we break the bars of the cage in which many women are confined with dreamlike unawareness? When will we grow up to become aware and awake to the shaping and molding brought about by being born a girl and go beyond the roles defined on the basis of being female? To grow up is to accept the wholeness of being in all facets of existence: body, mind, spirit, and culture.

Wife, mother, and daughter are traditional women's roles. All women are daughters, but not all women become wives or mothers. Today, more than ever, to become a wife or a mother involves intention and choice. Exercising intention and choice is tantamount to growing up. Realizing we are free to choose is the first step out of the cage.

One individual woman in the 21st century has the choice of staying in the cage or creating herself without cages. When she risks departing from cage roles, claiming her ability to strategize, invent, create, philosophize, or heal, she may be told directly or subtly that she is out of "her place." She may meet a wall of resistance, pushing her back to the traditionally defined roles of the cage.

Creation, not reaction, is the way to break the bonds. Creation and reaction are two words spelled with the same letters – change the "C," change the way you "see," and you will change your life. We see what we look for, not what we look at. Our own perspective is the basis for how we think, the emotions we experience, and the actions we take. Conscious awareness of our perspective is the key to self-creation.

We have come to the information age with the

growing probability that we are returning to a balance between right and left brainpower. Leonard Shlain optimistically proposes that the advent of photography in the last century and movies, television, and the Internet in this century are bringing our brains into better balance. Imagery and imagination are returning to real importance. With right brain traits becoming as important as left brain traits, with diplomacy instead of war, with the acceptance of emotional expression, and with the maturity of individual responsibility for sustaining all of life, we are becoming whole. Roles defined by gender are less the norm. Men are encouraged to participate fully in birthing and care of the young and all the joys of hearth and home. Women are now more visible as leaders in politics, religion, business, and professional life. Perhaps Shlain's theories are correct. The story is changing.

The characteristics of a conscious relationship, outlined by Harville Hendrix in *Getting the Love You Want*, are also the characteristics of a cage-free existence for both males and females. I have taken the liberty of restating these as permissions for any individual:

1. You can learn that your relationships have a

hidden purpose – the healing of your wounds from the past. This means that if you perceive yourself to be in a cage of limitations, you are following some old ancient or childhood pattern wounding. Those who would keep you in the cage are no less wounded.

2. You can learn to see more clearly, letting go of your illusions and empathetically understanding others and the world. You can ask yourself in every transaction with others, "Is this who I am?" or "Am I letting them define me?" You can define others more charitably. If they are not loving, you can assume they are asking for help.

3. You are capable of taking responsibility for communicating your needs and desires. You can tell your truth, without blame or judgment.

4. You can become more intentional in your interactions, rather than automatically following fight-flee-freeze-fix survival reactions. You can place the old brain more in the service of your neo-cortex rather than letting the primitive part of your thinking guide your actions.

5. You can learn to value the needs and wishes of others as highly as you value your own. Narcissistic victimization keeps you stuck. You are released from the bondage of the cage when you begin to think more about your capacity to give

begin to think more about your capacity to give with no strings attached.

6. You can search out, accept, and forgive your own dark side. Once you accept your negative qualities, you will not project them onto others. You will join the human race and not need to be a perfect god or goddess.

7. You can learn new ways to get your basic needs and desires met. Your independence can co-exist with intimacy. You can be with others in freedom.

8. You can find your own strength and develop your underdeveloped talents. Your talents are innate and your skills can be continually upgraded.

9. You can rediscover your loving nature and your desire to be whole. You can know that you are one with all life. You belong. You are wanted. You make a difference. You can contribute to a better world.

10. You can accept the difficulty of growing up.

ONE MORE THING

Although it may be difficult and seem counter-intuitive, the only response to those who would keep woman caged is the response of love, "for they know not what they do." Oppression comes from a base of fear, and this base of fear is the cage that imprisons men. It's important to remember that "perfect love casteth out fear." Our largest task is to learn how to love one another. We have no real choices other than peace, love, and compassion.

CHAPTER THREE

RAGES

*What obstructs our learning
to follow the path of love?*

When individual identity is based on gender or something that cannot change, there is a resulting accumulation of emotion toward that imprisonment. Emotions are not to be debated, denied, or masked. They must be given awareness and expression with appropriate safety measures.

Woman's rage may be greater than the rage of any other oppressed group, and more subtly expressed. Her rage is a silent river, buried deep in her conformity to the cages from which she gained her survival and her "place" in the human race.

RAGE AND POWER

No wonder we got mad! Accumulated oppression has affected women almost as if rage were a part of our DNA. All suppressed people react to

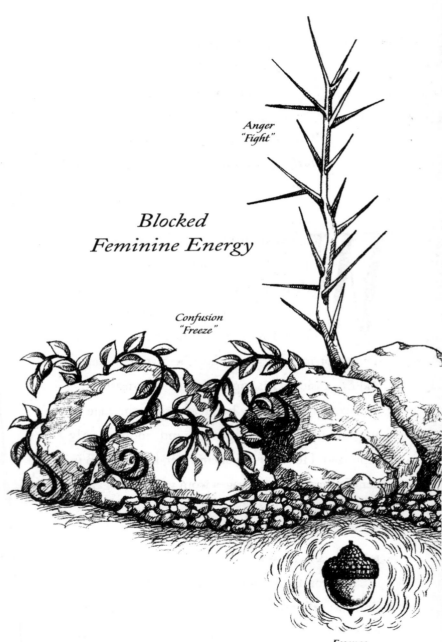

Anger
"Fight"

Blocked
Feminine Energy

Confusion
"Freeze"

Essence

their oppressors. When one woman "loses it" and begins to rage, she is swept into a river of rage. She dredges up all the past hurts and abuses, sometimes expressing them in very colorful language and behavior. This is pent up energy, having to do with sovereignty and power. For eons, woman couldn't claim her whole power as a decision-maker. Without dominion over her life or her body, woman learned to take power in subtle ways. She learned to be nice on the outside and seethe – perhaps unconsciously – on the inside. Her rage leaked out in various ways. She could hyperventilate. She could carp at her husband. She could have "the vapors." She could become suicidal. In the

Depression
"Flee"

Victorian era, she could faint. (With those wasp-waisted dresses and corsets, it was not difficult.) And as Ashley Montague asked, "What man could resist a woman in a supine position?"

Rage is a powerful source of energy. I have known women to dig flower beds, write books, scrub their houses and children, and move heavy furniture – all in motivational fits of rage. With such a prodigious amount of activity in motion, a great deal was accomplished. Much of that activity was beneficial, and, at least, the rage was dissipated.

There are many safe expressions that allow steam to be let off without homicide, suicide, or going crazy. Music often expresses our despair and anger. Melancholy, grief, and great sadness can be alleviated through song. Painting, sculpting, sports, dancing, and running are avenues of emotional expression that become potential rage reducers.

Sometimes one woman mobilizes a group to fight injustice or do good for society. Women working to preserve historic buildings, take back the streets, and build parks that are safe for children illustrate the motivation that is born of righteous indignation and focused anger. Women married to alcoholics sometimes get angry enough to act. In the world of addiction, the transformed rage of those recovering makes them available to others who need a helping hand or a loving friend. Young girls run away from home when abuse makes them angry enough to survive in a different way. All forms of abuse become transformational when the rage is contacted, expressed in safety, and allowed to become the new story with its powerful potential of healing. Anger can be a motivational, dynamic machine.

There is a story of a Buddhist monk in a Vietnamese monastery who held in his face the energy of his rage over his village being bombed for a third time. His anger was transformed into the energy he needed to mobilize the reconstruction of his village. The rage was the motivating force.

Emotional energy is fuel for change. We harm ourselves with our rage if we don't find an avenue for expression.

ANGER AND TRANSFORMATION

Anger is an outpouring of hot, negative emotion like a volcanic eruption. We look for someone or something to blame so that our self-pity is justified. In Adult Children of Alcoholics groups, we discover that our self-pity is the umbrella that covers our own core of shame, our fear that we may not be enough. Thus, our rage might be seen as a spilling-out of blame. When we blame, what we are and what happens to us are not our fault. We remain innocent, and innocence is perceived as the path to redemption. Our self-pity is the symptom of our basic self-view that we are not good enough.

To deny your anger is misguided, and to shame yourself for feeling sorry for yourself also is misguided. To look at our basic self-picture, which signals that we are not enough, and admit that the self-picture is not true, brings the possibility of awakening. What we need to do to overcome our rage is to get it clear in our own belief system that we are good enough. We are enough! We are more than enough!

Real change comes when the psychological defense mechanism called introjection is realized. Introjection allows us to believe that our oppressor is not at fault. At the unconscious level, when we introject, we internalize the characteristics of another person and cannot distinguish where we end and the other person begins. Somehow, we reason, if we were enough, we wouldn't be in this situation, so we are responsible – and guilty! Ending the introjection means facing the reality that the oppressor is different and separate from us. Then we can decide whether or not the oppressor is wrong.

This same emotional defense is used, unconsciously, by children of abusive or neglectful parents. Little children don't know their parents are not gods. They assume the big people are right. In like manner, women have not awakened to their innocence.

When we differentiate from the symbiosis of childhood, we move from being dependent on our parents to seeing ourselves as separate from our parents and interdependent. Typically, as adults, when we look for a cause of our dysfunction we blame our parents. In our outmoded cause-effect thinking, the perceived need to establish who or what is to blame is a dead end. Blaming one's parents is like singling out the carrier of infection that made us sick. It doesn't matter. We need to get well.

The therapy I experienced during the 1970s was based on discovery of the child within. Then came blaming the parents who wounded that child. I saw a lot of "me first" attitudes as a result. One patient actually sued his parents for parental malpractice. Identifying a scapegoat will not lead to healing. The real healing comes from inner strength. The process begins with a change in self-belief. The belief that we are "enough" becomes a rebirth. To follow such a belief is to become creative in our own right and to accept equal value in the world we inhabit.

I challenge all women to reject being victims and to realize their rightful responsibility for creating their own reality. The first revolutionary new belief to adopt is, "I am enough." For the Possible Woman, awareness and awakening to a change in self-belief means accepting that gender, established by birth, is not cause for caste assignment.

FORMULA FOR SUCCESS

Rage can be transformed to courage. In my work with women, I devised a formula for changed behavior that leads to positive growth. The formula has five factors: self-concept (SC), systems of support – one's relationships and environment (SS), goals and expectations – our intentions (G+E), time management (T), and energy management (E).

The formula may be expressed mathematically as:

$$Success = \frac{SC \times SS + (G+E)}{(T+E)}$$

Stated in words, the formula defines success as losing your anger by changing your basic self-identity. To achieve this, your self-concept – the essence of yourself – is multiplied by your systems of support added to goals and expectations. These three factors are divided by the ways in which we manage personal time and personal energy. Let's look at each element individually.

SELF-CONCEPT

In this age of information, we can further study the self within the individual. We have many methods for looking within, examining our feelings, obtaining therapy, or finding other forms of self-growth. Self-image, self-worth, self-discipline, self-consciousness, self-responsibility, self-direction, self-reliance, self-concept – ideas with roots in the 19th century transcendentalist movement – these are concepts of this century. Ours is the century of the self.

Self-awareness gave birth to a rising consciousness that allows us to know we exist. To experience the "I am-ness" – the existence of a good-enough self – means to recognize a little local self (not a big self, not a global self, but the essence of self that accepts boundaries and keeps on keeping on) as being capable of joy and spontaneous aliveness. We are a species of animal that has the capacity of mind to be aware of its own existence.

I remember the first time I discovered myself as a separate being. I was probably less than four years of age, sitting underneath the kitchen table on the linoleum floor in our farmhouse. I called to my mother, and she bent down and looked at me with a smile on her face. The thrill of knowing I was here and she was there is something I still remember. I felt included as one with everything but still separate unto myself. I experienced the thrill of existence – the great "I am."

How do you complete the statement, "I am...? Write at least 20 "I am" statements. Notice patterns in your self-descriptions.

Here are some examples:

I am a woman.

I am my mother's daughter.

I am happy.

I am full of wonder.

I am sometimes depressed.

I am frustrated.

I am a homemaker, chauffeur, hairdresser, laundress, secretary, volunteer, etc.

Notice how many of your sentences are completed with adjectives that describe you. How many are completed with nouns that identify you? How many express your unfulfilled longings? How many suggest your values? Let this list be a springboard for your self-awareness. From it you can begin to find self-acceptance and self-creation.

SYSTEMS OF SUPPORT

A positive self-concept is multiplied by a positive support system. Support systems are two-fold: the environment in which we live and the relationships we experience within that environment. To the level that both environment and relationships are positive, our self-concept grows more positive exponentially. To the level either environment or relationships are negative, self-concept is diminished or, at best, struggles to overcome the negative impact.

Look at your 20 "I am" statements. Which ones are negative identifiers? How can changing your support systems change your self-concept? How would you change your relationships? Your environment?

GOALS AND EXPECTATIONS

Goals are selected from our desires, the things we wish for, which represent possibilities for future goals. I recommend you keep an ongoing list of ninety or more wishes, written as declarative statements in present tense. Let these wishes define what success means to you. They can include tangible items you wish to have and intangibles that represent what you want to be.

My use of this concept became clear when I was considering earning my doctorate. My self-doubt and my fear of the risk were prevailing. I decided to place the wish on my list as a seed of potential. I remember the first time I wrote, "I am Marjorie R. Barlow, Ph.D.," and thought that would never be possible. I continued to write the sentence in my daily journal. The more I wrote the words, the more it seemed to be a possibility.

In a group therapy session I timidly announced my intention and desire to go back to school one more time (at age forty-five) and try for another degree. Within two weeks of my announcement, I was offered opportunities in two doctoral studies programs. I learned to never underestimate the power of words and the potency of self-declarations.

The wishes are similar to seeds a farmer selects to plant the next crop. Deciding to plant a wish is a choice made from the security of a good self-concept and good support. Once the choice is made, then the wish can sprout as a goal. Good nutrients, soil, water, air, and sunlight are necessary for a seed to germinate. For goals to be reached, similar nurturing and cultivation are necessary.

Write a list of everything you wished for as a child. Check off the items and accomplishments you have reached. For instance, as a child, I wished for a bicycle. My boyfriend gave me a bicycle when I was sixteen years old. So I can check that off the list. I wished for a beautiful house when I was growing up. I can now check off several houses. When you check it off, it has become yours ~ a goal now reached.

Write a second list of the things you wish for now. For at least three months, write your desires in great detail. These wishes can be for three different manifestations:

    1. *Qualities you wish to describe you;*

    2. *Accomplishments and achievements you wish to pursue; and*

    3. *Tangible things you wish to possess.*

In my goals workshops, I use seven words that begin with "r" to show the way to select a "wish" seed, plant it, wait for the harvest, and celebrate its fruition. The steps are:

1. Accept the right to have the goal;
2. Risk the changes the goal will bring;
3. Create readiness for the goal through taking responsibility for preparations;
4. Mentally rehearse having the goal through images, thoughts, words, and writing;
5. Relax and wait for the gestation of the goal;
6. Accept the reward when the goal is realized; and
7. Rejoice in celebration of the accomplishment of the goal.

When I look back on all those wish lists, I see

that it is true – we create our reality through our wishes, which become our goals, and our expectations concerning our goals.

Through this step-by-step method of goal achievement, I have many wishes that have become material realities. I received my Ph.D. degree shortly before my fiftieth birthday, and I spoke on a cruise ship two years ago. The gestation time for the Ph.D. was five years and for the cruise, ten years. For me, the most important "r" is "relax" – to be patient. Knowing that "I don't get what I say I want, I get what I expect," means to be vigilant to the ways I could sabotage myself. I may have said I wanted to speak on cruise ships, but for ten years, I probably didn't expect it could happen. Something in my deepest mind was still anchored in the self-concept that I couldn't do something so exotic. Most of all, I needed my own permission to fulfill my dream. I have learned to stay faithful to the mental rehearsal and not contaminate the process by my self-doubts and fears.

TIME

Each week, 168 clock hours of chronological time are given to us here on the planet Earth. How we manage that clock time is a factor in our success or lack of success.

The best time management technique is to manage time rather than task. Often when we look at the task, it seems too overwhelming and we begin to feel there is not enough time to do the task. If, however, we set a certain time each day to do that task and if, on that day, we do nothing in that time except that task, something amazing begins to happen. The task gets done! So prioritize the tasks, set a certain time in which you will address specific tasks, and keep your agreement to do that task at that time.

I once worked with a medical doctor who wanted to create a plan for managing the task of clearing his desk of mounds of paperwork. His procrastination was understandable since the task appeared too large. He made a plan that involved his arriving at the office thirty minutes earlier than his usual time. He asked his receptionist to hold that time sacred – no coffee, phone calls, or visiting – for doing the task. To his surprise, his paperwork was finished within a week!

At the soul's level, time is timeless. When time seems to be the problem, it is useful to claim one's infinite spirit, eternal and ongoing. To let go of one's time constraints and simply "be" for a few seconds returns us to equanimity. My Aunt Jimmie told me she dealt with her worries by saying, "We won't know this is a problem in a hundred years."

ENERGY

One secret for using energy is to be creative, not reactive. It means much more than merely rearranging the spelling of the words. Motivation is rarely a problem when the creative juices are flowing. To be creative means we are proactive in our use of time and energy. This means growing up enough to be in charge of our own beliefs, perspective, thoughts, feelings, and behavior. This maturity risks being wildly successful. Risk, readiness, responsibility, and getting into one's own flow will open up further possibilities of creating an exciting existence.

The same creative energy can be negatively drained into reactive anger and dissipated toward some outside event or person over which we have no control. Holding the energy and using it in the interest of some self-chosen creation is transformative as well as beneficial. The organization Mothers

Against Drunk Driving (MADD) is a good example of the transformation of rage that came from the tragedy of lost life. These mothers transformed the energy of their rage to bring social awareness and cultural possibilities of change for the better.

Without overt, mainstream empowerment, any woman can get very angry. When angry, she will find ways to accomplish her mission through manipulations or she will burn herself out or up, destroying her boring or abusive world. A woman must be cautious to not get so full of rage that she forgets the path of the heart. She could become militant and turn into an imitation warrior-male or become adamantly anti-male. Her strength does not lie in that direction, nor will her transformation – those ways simply echo the past.

Too many women I have worked with in therapy are caught up in blaming men for their condition. No single male is to blame. Blaming, faultfinding, or establishing a cause is not the way to cure the effect. This must be something new and very different. Transforming rage into courage, using our energy for creation rather than reaction means we might learn to care about our world. Forgiveness is easier when we see the enemy as the same as us, when we can see ourselves projected into the other(s) who brought the harm. They, too, are wounded. We might then begin to love one another. Then we will have taken the path of the heart. The path of the heart is the path of success.

Let go of your rage for your sake. To do so, you must first be in a safe environment to express your anger. Second, you will need time to discover and express it. To let go of rage, write out your old leftover angers toward individuals from your past, to institutions, cultures, and all sources of the limitations imposed upon you just because you were born female. Remember any time you were excluded, made invisible, taken for granted, abused, used, exploited, dishonored, or devalued. Experience these feelings. Express them through writing, shouting, talking, screaming, painting, dancing, and safely beating up something. Third, be aware you need not get revenge. The goal of this exercise is not to change someone else or teach her or him a lesson; it is to let go of your destructive rage and allow it to be transformed. After all, if someone else made a mistake, why should you still suffer? Fourth, realize the energy behind your rage can be transformative for your personal world as well as the world at large.

In the world view of action and reaction, other ideas can be considered. Other species and our environmental resources have received poor treatment. Parallel to the story of woman and her mistreatment through the ages is the larger story of how we have used and abused our natural resources. Mother Nature may one day express her rage concerning what we have done to destroy the thin covering of topsoil and the delicate thin skin of atmosphere here on this planet. The smaller story of women's journey is a mirror for the larger story of the journey of planet Earth.

CHAPTER FOUR

PAGES

The expansion of the mind through learning is a vital component in the story of the Possible Woman.

There was a time when thinking, research, engineering, and writing itself were considered primarily masculine in nature. Theology, art, science, and philosophy were male endeavors. Men played the parts of females on stage. Female composers and writers were not heard or read. Woman, connected to nature from the beginning, did necessary work that did not require education. Necessary work included the feeding, cleaning, and tending of the population. Women were not regarded as able to think in complex abstractions or able to conduct banking or commerce. All too common was a general attitude in which no real effort was made to help women learn to read beyond a rudimentary level.

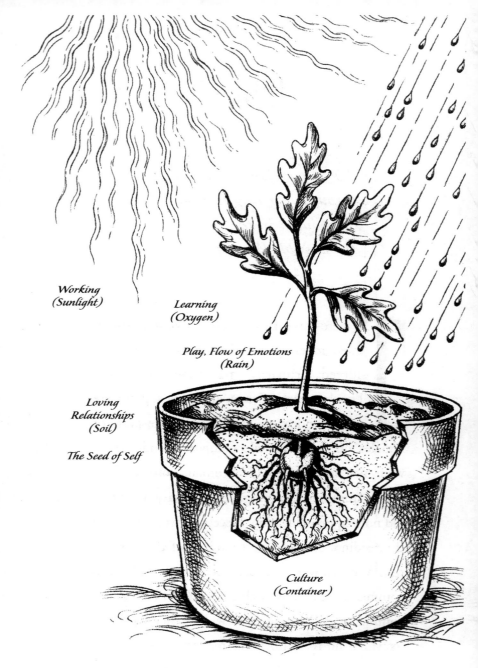

Working
(Sunlight)

Learning
(Oxygen)

Play, Flow of Emotions
(Rain)

Loving
Relationships
(Soil)

The Seed of Self

Culture
(Container)

Pathway of Growth

I have met women who were not permitted a college education, though their brothers were. Parents rationalized that a daughter would marry and be supported by her husband, so college would be wasted time and effort. One father supported his logic by pointing out his daughter's failure to comprehend mathematics, suggesting she could never pass college algebra. The unspoken implications were that women could not be independent or take care of themselves, that household management could be done by unskilled labor, and that an education was not important if one were a wife or mother.

Today girls are given more opportunities. Women are more free to partake of knowledge, and with their agile brains and their ability to multi-track, women are learning. Female children in Western cultures have the opportunity to read, write, paint, make music, dance, create beauty, and express themselves. As authors, poets, researchers, writers, and journal keepers, women contribute. Through written pages, woman blossoms. Through her reading and her studying, woman is cultivating her own power.

Men need not be the model nor the enemy. However, the differences between male and female are not the points to emphasize. The unique spirit of the feminine is the point.

In the old paradigm, communities were organized around the ancient precepts, concepts, and values that emphasized the biological differences between men and women. Helen Luke in *The Way of Woman* says, "Those who assert that the only difference between men and women is biological, and that in every other way they are equal, have the same inborn potentialities, have disastrously missed the point. Equality of value between individuals is an eternal truth, beyond all comparisons, whereas 'superior' and 'inferior' are relative terms defining abilities or degrees of consciousness." Luke goes on to say, "A woman is born to be essentially and wholly a woman and the more deeply and consciously she is able to know and live the spirit, the Logos, within her the more surely she will realize the truth."

In another passage, Luke states that woman can flourish while, "maintaining her roots in her basic feminine nature – that which receives, nourishes, and gives birth on all levels of being through her awareness of the earth and her ability to bring up the water of life from under the earth. All her true creativeness in every aspect of her life, private or public, springs from this."

Jean Shinoda Bolen challenges assumptions traditionally held in psychology in her book, *Goddesses in Everywoman*. Two respected grandfathers of the science of psychology, Sigmund Freud and C. G. Jung, saw women as inferior males. Freud theorized that women were envious of the anatomy of males. Jung, in a kinder vein, said that women were not inherently defective but that they were less creative and less able to be objective or take decisive action than men. Bolen states that women used to be unconscious of the powerful effects that social steroetypes had on them. She further says that women may not be awake to the powerful forces within them that influence what they do and how they feel. Her book describes a new psychological perspective of women based on images of women that have stayed alive in human imagination for hundreds of years. Seven archetypal goddesses, or personality types, reveal the patterns women follow today. (For more information on exploring goddess archetypes, see the "Possible

Woman Workshop" in Appendix A.)

Every woman has the leading role in her life story. Understanding the mythic dimensions of her story will help any woman move in the direction of her individuality and her wholeness. The first step is to awaken from the unconscious stereotypes. One sure way to awaken is through the avenue called learning.

In my work with women, I have witnessed many positive life changes through return to education. I have met women who have found refuge from abuse in battered women's shelters after leaving home in the middle of the night to escape the threat of violence. Some have enrolled in college. Other women, whose children are now grown, return to complete the degree that was interrupted when they married. I know several retired women who recently have studied creative writing, theology, art, or computer science.

Women learn quickly and remember accurately. Girl babies talk earlier than boy babies do; they walk earlier, they have more words to say, and they learn more readily in school. Reading tests in elementary schools tend to show higher scores for girls. In the last fifty years, girls were high achievers in school until they reached puberty. But after age twelve, their scores in science and math were lower than those of boys. To remain in the mainstream of male-oriented curricula required strong motivation. More recently, women have been encouraged to study math and science. College programs help older students returning to earn a degree. Women's studies has found a prominent place in university curricula. Opportunity is available.

If the Possible Woman is to be realized, she needs to learn. Traditional learning is done through reading and writing. Pages, therefore, become important key tools to growth and development. Education is the door we pass through to break out of traditional female roles and enter the world of possibilities.

KEEPING JOURNALS AND DIARIES

A little girl writing in her diary is a traditional picture of female childhood, and writing is a wonderful way to achieve self-awareness and self-expression. Writing can be a therapeutic healing mechanism. To keep a journal is my first assignment to any client seeking self-development. Julia Cameron's book, *The Artist's Way*, is a useful guide.

One of Cameron's suggestions is "writing the morning pages." Filling three pages every morning is an excellent tool for developing self-awareness.

Self-development is the task of our aliveness. We are filled with a life force. We want to thrive (which is more than mere survival) and to experience our aliveness. We are conscious beings with the urge to express that aliveness. In the spiral of growth that we climb throughout one lifetime, self-awareness leads to self-expression. Through self-expression, a form begins to emerge that is the essence of being. Essence is the core of the true self. Writing is a path for any woman who wants to experience and express the essence of the Possible Woman within.

THERAPY AS EDUCATION

My own work with women reveals many stories of women released to find their true selves through the process of psychotherapy. One Possible Woman in the 1970s was Gloria (not her real name). Gloria was widowed at age fifty-two. Her family brought her to me because she had become agoraphobic. Agoraphobia means, literally, the fear of the marketplace. In Gloria's case, being agoraphobic meant she would not leave her home except under the most extreme conditions, such as going to the doctor if she were ill, with much protection and coaxing. Her children dreaded the ordeal of helping her go outside her home.

Gloria's psychotherapy amounted to cognitive re-structuring, which is a form of healing through thought awareness and control. Her thoughts and beliefs were so limiting and confining that she lived in a constant state of anxiety, worry, and fear. I taught her the process of Self Re-Parenting described in the "Stages" chapter. Gloria learned about her own internal Parent, Adult, and Child ego states. She learned that her internal Parent could protect and help her internal frightened Child. She faced her irrational beliefs and learned to calm herself from within. Her therapy required patience from herself and from me. Eventually, Gloria was able to take charge of her thoughts and give herself the comfort she needed to venture out into the larger world outside her house. Soon she had garnered enough courage to begin to drive a car, which helped her children in many good ways. Over a period of two years, she transformed her life from the inside out. She studied for and obtained her GED, proudly receiving her high school diploma, and found work as a receptionist. In a short time, she found a new male friend with whom she built a new life of pleasure and productivity. Her changes were profound. Through education, therapy, and the support of her children, Gloria created a new life.

Eugenia was a very intelligent young woman in her early thirties when she arrived at my office. Her dilemma had to do with being torn between the demands of her husband and small children and her overeating. She said, "I look for comfort foods. I get restless and want to run away." At night, she was tired and listless. She and her husband had drifted into a routine of work, tend to children and necessary things, sleep, eat, and work again. When she began to look at her life and plan what she wished to change, she knew that her unfinished degree was a source of shame. Over the course of several weeks, Eugenia focused on herself and began to accept the value and need for self-caretaking. Her husband was cooperative and urged her to "get out of the house." One way she could do that was to take a class in creative writing at the local junior college. She felt free to do that because her husband was involved in the emotional and physical care and feeding of the children, and she trusted that her absence would not harm her family. She began to recover her wellspring of creativity and her joy in life. Her exit interview was a quiet recitation of what she had come through. She remembered the days of despair and quiet desperation as a time she described as slow death. Her new interests had brought happiness back to her marriage and the light of hope to her future. Instead of feeling "taken for granted," Eugenia knew she was an acknowledged contributor to her world at home and the larger world of her community. She began teaching a course in journaling at her church. Her latest plan is to return to school with the intention of completing her degree in journalism.

Rosa and Tom came to counseling for the purpose of deciding whether to stop her career to have their first child. Her biological clock was ticking, and she felt the conflict of what she would lose in the years given to the secure parenting of their baby. They both were agreed that childcare was essentially best done by the parents, but their lifestyle required they both earn as much as possible. Their time in my office was an educational research project for them. They were in uncharted territory, rewriting the book on how to live in this age. They worked through many hypotheses:

1. Either of them could stay home and be the full-time caretaker.

2. They could take one job between them (both were trained social workers), buy a camper for their truck, park it near the office, and both tend the child, guaranteeing the social work agency that one job could be covered by both of them.

3. They could move her parents into their home as live-in caretakers.

4. They could move to the country, live off the land, and get back to the basics of life without modern conveniences.

Tom and Rosa worked diligently to explore the practicalities of each possibility and eventually combined aspects of all four ideas. They sold their city condo and moved to the country, her parents moved to an adjoining property, *and* they opened their own social work agency, contracting to do a drug prevention and treatment program for their county. Tom said that they did the equivalent work of an advanced degree in the research, the brainstorming, and the fine tuning of their relationship. He called it a "Ph.D. in Creative Living." Both were enthusiastic and ready for the birth of their baby girl the following year. They had created a new life with the visionary capacities of their open minds.

SELF-EXPRESSION TODAY

Computers bring a new dimension to the pages we write. From the time of Gutenberg's invention of the printing press in the 15th century to the year 2000, we have experienced a shock of possibilities for self-expression. Emily Dickinson's poems were handwritten on paper, tied with ribbons, and stored in hatboxes. Today's poets can store volumes on hard disks. Any woman can write, edit, and publish her story in her own home. With appropriate equipment, she need only speak her story into permanent, printable storage.

Global communication is possible for anyone. The communications explosion has opened our minds to new realities. Telephone service, fax machines, and the Internet enable worldwide contact and instant communication – a future-shock-wave of heretofore unheard of proportions. Our grandparents couldn't imagine computer games, chat rooms, resources at the touch of a key, and instant knowledge of world events. One ten-year-old today knows and responds to more than our grandparents conceived of or comprehended in one lifetime. Where is it taking us? What is the global meaning for the people of planet Earth? Perhaps we are preparing to live in space. Or maybe we are evolving into a different species. How does this affect women? My primary concern is the impact of the information age on human relating.

The communication explosion affects relationships between the generations and committed love relationships. It seems easy to relate to a new friend who becomes a fantasy lover through the seeming intimacy of e-mail. When you can become ageless, weightless, faceless, and nameless, you can begin a wonderful new identity. The e-mail partner can do the same, and the romantic overtones are limitless. By comparison, a real-life partner seems crass and uncaring, if not disgusting, in his or her everyday, mono-dimensional self.

In my practice, I've dealt with several cases of marital discord that arose because of relationships that began in chat rooms on the Internet. One woman with a successful husband and a good life filled with volunteer work, church, friends, and the symbols of success became bored. Through the Internet, she escaped boredom, found someone exciting, and fell in love. Her whole life turned upside down, and she was in an agony of indecision. Stay or go? The surprise to her was that she could be so completely smitten. As the story moved on, the couple ended their marriage. The Internet relationship is still confused and unresolved. We live in changing times.

SHOWING UP

In this, the information age, woman is ready, and she will show up. Her time is now. The evolutionary infrastructure is in place. The apprenticeship is finished. The eons of training have prepared her. She has something to contribute. She can build relationships. She can learn. She can communicate. She can process information. Whether it is on the pages she studies or the pages she writes, in the political arena where she uses the force of her personality, or in the arts, the sciences, or the corporate community, woman is ready to be fully existent. To do that, we must know ourselves and be aware of what we like. We need to discover where we show up in the world at our best. We need to know what motivates us.

Whenever I think about what gives me pleasure, I discover once again how much I love to read. In my childhood, I read labels, magazines, catalogues, and all the books that were in our country school library. I am full of excitement when I read the ideas found on the pages of good books. I admire those who can communicate through the written word. I am in awe of authors who can hold their readers in suspense. Writing, for me, is not easy. I read far more than I write. My nightstand holds books waiting for my night reading. I read on airplanes, in cars, and as I wait in line at banks. I confess to reading books as I drive cross-country. The books I am reading are akin to good friends; when I place them on my bookshelf, they wait for me to return for a visit. I learned from my husband the value of choosing a book at random and opening to a page for a brief respite. I never fail to find some nugget of inspirational gold.

Browsing in bookstores is great recreation for me. It was in one of my indulgent visits to a good bookstore that I discovered Angeles Arriens' writings. I especially like her *Four-Fold Way: Walking the Paths of the Warrior, Teacher, Healer, and Visionary*, in which she expounds four rules for living. They are:

1. Show up, in full mind, body, and spirit;

2. Tell your truth, without blame or judgment;

3. Follow the path of the heart; and

4. Stay open to outcomes.

These four principles are simple truths to follow as you pursue learning.

Self-expression is the best way to show up. Self-awareness reveals the truth we need to tell, without blame or judgment. Self-love reveals the path of the heart. And self-knowledge opens up the possibility of learning without becoming attached to outcomes. These principles invite each Possible Woman to enter the world with her own personality and the force of her unique talents.

Whether the endeavor is a corporation or a country, woman brings the fresh, new possibility of partnership on an equal basis instead of the old dominance-conquest model. Woman can be in community. Woman's leadership is naturally able to establish teaching-learning communities. The Possible Woman is the original servant leader, one who is dedicated to the development of those around her rather than controlling those who work for her. She, as servant leader, is interested in growth rather than domination and power. A servant leader does what is necessary. She is an excellent listener and has the trust of her employees. She grooms her replacement, and she fosters leadership. She may make coffee, carry water to the workers, and fill in when the work demands. She is valuable to her organization wherever she serves.

MAKING CHOICES

All learning involves choice and being aware that we have choice. We choose a college major, a career, a spouse, what we eat, where we live. How we choose speaks to our basic life mission, which is not martyrdom or subservience, but that which fosters the common good. Ashley Montague, in *Growing Young*, describes ideal qualities of the human being, one of which is compassionate intelligence. A brilliant mind is not enough, he says. Montague advocates that good intelligence must be used with compassion, not for power or dominance. The word itself, compassion, suggests we have passion in common. We are connected.

I believe three things are necessary for compassionate intelligence. First, some code of *morality* that implies the cultivation of virtue or a basic concept of what fosters the good of self, others, and society. Second, a belief in one's own *worthiness* is essential to making behavioral choices that reflect that code of morality without doing harm. Third, the *awareness* and self-direction of one's own beliefs, thoughts, feelings, and behavior are necessary for self-responsibility.

The following exercise lets you examine your life, getting to the heart of these ideas. Write your own answers to these questions. Keep the writing. Answer the questions again next year at this same time. Then write more pages concerning the changes you have made or not made. Continue writing about your thoughts and beliefs until you are clear about what limits you.

Am I being who I want to be? Why or why not?

Do I love and approve of myself? Why or why not?

Am I creating my world and my life in accord with my own ethics? Why or why not?

*Am I choosing what I desire to learn in congru-
ence with my morality? Why or why not?*

My clients often express irrational beliefs that
seem to fly in the face of answering "yes" to these
questions. They seem to live as if they believe:

I can't be who I want to be because...

I can't love and approve of myself until...

I could create my world and my life if... or
when...

I am unable to choose my own path of learning
because...

These beliefs show up in thoughts that
support, with rationalization and justifications, the
impossibility of change. Change is the one
common element consistently present in your life.
Change is not impossible, it is inevitable.

All change begins with awareness. Once you
are aware that you think in a certain way, you can
take charge of and change your thoughts. For
example, if I truly believe that I cannot write well,
I will think this without knowing if it is true. To
change, I must raise to conscious level the idea that
I seem to be following a thought or belief that may
not be true. Then I can make declarative state-

ments (in positive terms, in present tense) that are true to what I want to create. These are called affirmations. Every time I become aware of a negative thought in reference to my writing, I can return to my affirmation. In this way, I can reprogram my mind.

Write a list of declarative sentences, expressing new beliefs that you desire to adopt. Notice how you react internally to each sentence. Be patient with your resistance to change. Continue to declare the new belief. As an example, I am using affirmations to change my old belief that writing is not easy for me. My affirmation is "I am writing a book easily and cheerfully." To overcome my self-doubt about my writing, my affirmation is "I am writing an interesting and engaging book."

Until we change our beliefs about self, we will continue to show up in old behaviors. We can work on changing behavior through changing reinforcements. We can express emotions and receive a change of feeling. We can restructure our thoughts and change our imagery. Ultimately, we need to change our beliefs. Beliefs about ourselves as women in this world and beliefs about our relationships with others, women or men, can change and are changing. Learning about connectedness and about self is the path to change. To grow, to evolve, to become spontaneously alive, and to express that aliveness is possible. I believe it is inevitable. We have reached the critical mass. We are ready. Our time is now.

My personal experience has convinced me that I must continue to read, to learn, and to apply what I learn if I am to change my old self-image. I have found that I thrive when I keep my mind infused with ideas and thoughts that contradict the detrimental, limiting programming of my childhood. Therefore, I continue to read, to study, and to meditate and pray about what I am reading. These activities guide my thinking out of the morass of old damaging self-beliefs. Words are powerful. Affirmations – written, read, or spoken – are essential to self-transformation. Words on pages can awaken us to the joys of lifelong learning.

THE POWER OF WORDS

The prevailing belief at the turn of the last

century that continues to some extent even to this day is that men are the real and true human beings and women are secondary, dependent "helpmates." Most studies of human learning have been conducted for "man as a species," with the expectation that woman would automatically include herself in the references to "mankind." Women were considered "incorrect" and "too sensitive" if they didn't feel included in the study of "man." These strongly held beliefs found their origin and justification in the belief that God is male.

A minister of the Christian religion reported to me a story from his time in seminary. Some female ministerial students objected to the maleness of the language used in the Bible and the worship services. The male ministerial students insisted that it didn't matter, since the word man included woman. The female preachers persisted and eventually offered to conduct daily chapel services using all female pronouns, referring to "God the Mother," etc. The men insisted this would not make a difference. So for several weeks, feminine pronouns were consistently used at services. References were made to "God, in her infinite wisdom," and the language of the liturgy was changed to eliminate masculine references. Many men found themselves indisposed at chapel time – they reported bad colds, sore throats, diarrhea, nausea, headaches, and other stress-related illnesses. They were not lying; they were truly, physically ill. The female language with the godhead as feminine provoked a gigantic shift in male consciousness. And the shift provoked changes in their physical being.

When God was perceived as the fertile feminine life force, the cycles of growth were understood through the reproductive patterns of the plant and animal kingdoms. (Technology, industry, and scientific understanding brought us to a more mechanical explanation of life cycles.) Now that we communicate through left brain words, God is perceived to be masculine. Perceptions create the reality we experience. Our social conditioning is based on these perceptions.

A social paradigm is the vision of reality around which a community organizes itself. The old social paradigm held beliefs of a mechanical model of the universe, the human body as a machine, cultures competing for power, unlimited exploitation of the Earth as a resource, and the belief that a society in which the female is everywhere subsumed under the male is one that follows a basic law of nature. In his book *The Web of Life*, Fritjof Capra describes the new paradigm in which all life is interconnected. "Ultimately," Capra writes, "deep ecological awareness is spiritual or religious awareness. When the concept of the human spirit is understood as the mode of consciousness in which the individual feels a sense of belonging, of connectedness, to the cosmos as a whole, it becomes clear that ecological awareness is spiritual in its deepest essence."

Inside every woman is a powerful feminine spirit that is no longer able to be kept silent. Woman can find her voice, accept the truth of the feminine way, speak and write her words, and change the world. We live in exciting times! Our new myth is born out of our past.

CHAPTER FIVE

STAGES

"All the world's a stage,
And all the men and women
merely players...."

William Shakespeare
As You Like It

The drama of one individual life lived on the world stage unfolds in stages. Stage is a word with twofold meaning. If the individual is born female, her stages of life are reflective of her as a girl and as a woman. She is "on stage," living through various stages of development. Each stage of her development is one scene or one act in her life drama, her play.

WORLD DRAMA

One person's life drama is part of a larger production. The drama unfolds with changing roles for women. In the present age of creativity and communion, woman is able and ready to claim her highest good for the good of the Earth. Restoration of the Earth requires cooperation of all

Stages of Growth

Self-Reliant

Self-Worthy

Self-Directing

Self-Responsible

Self-Starting

Self-Creating

Self-Contributing

the characters on the world stage.
Woman embodies the Great Mother,
the nurturer and sustainer of life. Women have the
capacity and the ability to bring cooperation and
collaboration. The world drama is changing. The
new scene includes changes for individual human
beings, and women in particular.

WOMEN'S STAGES

The spiral of growth and development for
one individual female has always been physical,

psychological, relational, and spiritual. Each brings with her the collective experience of all the females who have ever lived. Our physical bodies are alike, and our psychological flow is similar. We live in relationship, and our journey has many commonalties. Journalist Cokie Roberts wrote about this in her book, *We Are Our Mothers' Daughters*, when she described her visit to a tiny museum in Marathon, Greece: "Here the objects from the everyday lives of women from thousands of years ago overwhelmed me with their familiarity. I could have opened the cases, put on their jewels, and taken up their tools, picked up where they left off without a moment's hesitation. ...We are connected throughout time and regardless of place. We are our mothers' daughters."

Of course, each woman also lives her own individual, unique set of experiences. These experiences evolve through stages, as well.

BLOOD MYSTERIES AND EMOTIONS

Consider first the female body and its physical stages. The great mystery of the womb is part of her heritage as a woman (womb-man). The nature of any female's major difference from her male counterpart lies in her physical body and its uniqueness.

Examine your personal story and its progress through the ancient blood mysteries. Before 5,000 B.C., women, fertility, and birth were held in high honor, and a woman was a treasure held in awe and respect. Fertility in plants and animals was treated with reverence. The maiden, the mother, and the crone were three stages all women experienced. As the maiden, a young woman was waiting to fulfill her function as a mother. Her menstrual flow ushered in her second stage, motherhood. It was believed she saved her blood to make a baby. In menopause, she saved her blood to make wisdom. How would your life be different if you felt this honor and reverence for your body and its capabilities?

My Women's Wisdom Group, which began twenty years ago, has included hundreds of women for brief or extended membership. Most of the members are mothers, but some have not borne children. Some have already completed a natural menopause; others have had surgical menopause through hysterectomy. Several are in their Wise Old Woman (WOW) stage. Through the group, these remarkable women discover a spiritual High Self that offers the acceptance, nurturing, caring, and interest that all women deserve. They express beliefs, thoughts, sensations, feelings, and behavior by talking with warmly accepting group members and through writing, dancing, art, or music.

The important idea here is to express, and the expressing cannot be done except in an atmosphere of safety. Here are the ground rules:

1. Each woman gets a turn to speak.

2. No one is coerced into speaking; you can take your turn by choosing not to speak.

3. The other group members respond to what you have to say with respectful interest and non-judgmental listening.

4. Through unconditional acceptance – the absence of judgment, advice-giving, and second-guessing – an atmosphere of safety is created. (Safety disappears under conditions of criticism or judgment.) Members may reflect on what was said or respond with empathy and validation.

5. Members honor time, stay with subjects they bring, and don't gossip.

The women who come to the Wisdom Group are sometimes in despair. They have been abandoned or rejected by lovers, husbands, and/or families. Some have been abused – sexually, emotionally, physically, or spiritually. Others have simply led quiet lives of desperation and dependency, like the woman with five children who is the wife of a recovering alcoholic and depends on his sobriety. They may have been passed over for promotion at work. Some are single parents, rearing families alone. Almost all of them have problems with the flow of money. Even the ones who have inherited great wealth have money problems. Happiness, for them, is often based on happenings, events, or other conditions outside themselves. A continuous wellspring of joy seems elusive. Discouragement and depression, anger and anxiety that accompany life in crisis are what we hear from these very able, brilliant females. Yet each one has a resonant, radiant life force that sustains her. In this, the members of the Women's Wisdom Group represent all women.

AWAKENING

Where can each woman begin on her road of awakening the radiant life force within? Physical development and caring for her body seem to be the best beginning for any woman in need of recovering or building her self-esteem. Just as the first stage of physical development is infancy, with necessary attention to food, rest, sleep, safety, and comfort, so a woman can return to self-care of her body at the basic level as a way of inviting her awakening. When women give their bodies respect and protection through good nutrition, healthy exercise, and adequate rest, self-worth moves toward the positive.

Physically, we can see changes and know about ourselves through weight, height, and other mechanical measurements. We can know ourselves as we progress through physical life stages from menarche to menopause, but what about our psyche and its development? What are the tasks of growth in stages of life in the non-physical dimension?

Much of what our culture accepts about development comes largely from the work of two men, Sigmund Freud and Erik Erikson. Freud defined psychosexual stages of development. From the oral, oral exploratory, anal, genital, latency, to teen identity, the emerging sexuality of the child was a prime force in the development of self-concept. Girl children were programmed to meet the demands of the roles of female sexual identity and tribal mores. By the time she reached puberty, a woman had the possibility of a limited script that directed her to be wife, mother, and support person.

Erikson's eight psychosocial stages of man have been taught in university classes for decades. Erikson's stages have been questioned as valid for everyone because they were based on a limited, mostly male sample. In his second stage, for example, he believed two-year-olds learn autonomy or shame, but even at that age female children have been observed to move to a caretaking, self-invisible role that's hardly autonomous. Their branching away from the accepted norm at this young age can be seen as a response to the social programming assigned to girls. Little boys, instead, were given the wide-open possibility of climbing the growth ladder with societal affirmation of their will, competence, loyalty, and a caring place in the commercial world. Their way was assured as a way of independence. In academia and eventually in the marketplace, male children were conditioned to achieve. They arrived at old age with a sense of worth and acceptability. Women, ironically, just seemed to age.

An individual can be programmed, psychologically, by the age of eleven, to have a self-concept of inferiority or inadequacy. The child's progress may have been shaped into fear, shame, guilt, and a sense of limitation just because she is female. Infant girls receive parental attention faster when they cry, and parents comfort little girls more often than little boys. The implication is that she is delicate, weak, and needs help sooner. Girls excel in all subjects until they reach middle school. They then move away from the sciences, math, and sports achievement. Sports programs for girls and women receive less recognition and less funding. As professionals, women athletes earn far less money. Changes in this social programming are on the horizon as more women rise to positions of management and power. Childhood and adolescence for girls today are less limited.

The time since World War II and the social changes of the 60s brought liberation to females beyond their sexual roles and expectations. Women now enter a new century with the probability of fifty years of life beyond menopause. Their stages of development are not simply limited to their sexuality. The pure power of that knowledge results in the profound truth that woman can look to far more than mere diversification in her development.

POSSIBLE WOMAN LIFE STAGES

Woman is, by nature, relational. The roles of daughter, wife, and mother are relational roles. Sister, aunt, niece, and grandmother are relational. (In fact, all human interaction requires relationship talent.) Understanding her relational stages can help a woman to understand herself and her growth and development. Through relationships, the Possible Woman emerges.

SEVEN LIFE STAGES

The seven life stages for the Possible Woman represent innate capacities that can be developed intentionally as abilities. While these stages are descriptive for both males and females, they especially describe the potential of each individual woman. They are: first, the optimism of being *Self-Starting*; second, the will to be *Self-Responsible*; third, the purpose to be *Self-Directing*; fourth, the enthusiasm to be *Self-Worthy*; fifth, the confidence to become *Self-Reliant*; sixth, the satisfaction of being *Self-Contributing*; and seventh, the joy of being *Self-Creating*.

STAGE 1 — SELF-STARTING

With a safe, serene, and non-violent womb experience, a little girl arrives in the world with the capability to relate, to reach out, to self-generate her own radiance. She holds a sense of trust in the world that is based on her healthy gestation and birth. Her survival is assured. She can enter life. Her life force is propelled into being. Since her existence is assured, she expands into optimism and hopefulness. She is set to thrive, not just survive.

The negative possibility of this stage is that a little girl may actually come into life at her birth with a sense of distrust and fear. She may already have received, in utero, prejudicial attitudes about being female. The ambience of the home and the attitudes of the mother *and* the father have a great deal to do with the emotional security of a gestating baby. The experience of birth, gentle or violent, also shapes her emotional well-being.

The drive to grow and the ability to be self-starting are being born even as the infant is being born. The life force cannot be stopped, but it can be hampered, even damaged. In the early months of an infant girl's life, she is symbiotic and attached to her caretakers. From her helpless, dependent, infant state, she can be responsibly nurtured into a human being with emotional security.

Just as seeds in nature, when planted in good soil and given nutrients, air, water, and sunlight, will grow into the plant the seed was destined to be, so it is with human beings. One individual girl child needs the human equivalent of air, water, sunlight, and good soil so that she can grow into the expanded version of her true self. The drive to grow is there and cannot be denied. In the middle ages, Meister Eckhardt said that pear trees grow from pear seeds. Humans, he said, are God-Seeds. We are created in the image and likeness of God. We grow from God-Seed to God-Self, given an environment and relationships that nurture our growth through each developmental stage.

STAGE 2 — SELF-RESPONSIBLE

The parents' responsibility to the baby girl's needs in these first two years, when she is learning so much, establishes in her a reliance on the security and safety of her home surroundings.

Responsive parent behaviors are a model she will emulate throughout her life. The self-response-able Possible Woman was nurtured adequately and protected in the first eighteen months of her life outside the womb.

The human infant needs a much longer gestation time inside the safe haven of the mother's body than does the infant of most other animals. But since her brain is so large with a skull-case to accommodate the size, the baby must move outside the mother's body to continue growing after nine months. Humans are somewhat like marsupials, needing the pouch following the womb. Responsible parenting furnishes that "pouch" and models and fosters responsible children who are emotionally secure. As the baby girl begins to sense herself separate from her caretakers, she reaches out to explore her world. She crawls, she toddles, and she runs, and wise parents are warmly available. They respond to her explorations with encouragement coupled with sensitive protection. The toddler girl is practicing responsiveness and response-ability as she follows her curiosity.

The negative side of this stage comes to girl babies when parents are less than responsive to her needs, or when they become intrusively responsible for her every bodily function. Her body, treated like an object, can become a source of shame. She will begin to build on the fear and become vigilant toward her caretakers. This stage includes governance of the body. Little girls learn sphincter control, which includes eye blinking and mouth movements as well as defecation and urination. Well-meaning parents may send shaming messages that she is flawed and that they somehow have to mold her and redeem her. Power struggles between parent and child develop around control issues.

STAGE 3 — SELF-DIRECTING

Our little girl has now reached the pre-school play age, her third and fourth years of life. She is becoming an individual in her own right, with a strong sense of beingness. Her core self is positively internalized, and she is now in a position to grow the woman within the girl. Her sense of worth is unquestioned because her parents are able to reflect her transient identities instead of judging and directing her every action. Internally, she is sure of herself and can express who she is. She has the basic building blocks of knowing she will survive and be

safe, and her self-esteem is solid as an internal construct. Her identity is forming through her process
of experimentation.

In the negative scenario, she may already be
building the habit of feeling guilty and inadequate,
with a hovering, awful, worrisome cloud of damp-
ened self-worth. Vigilant, directive parenting, with
too much intrusion and interference with her ideas
and choice making, sends the message of her guilt.
Well-meaning parents are trying to give her an
identity, formed from their own ideals, instead of
encouraging her to experiment with who she is.
While it may be hard to believe, all these elements
of her future life are happening long before she
goes to school.

STAGE 4 — SELF-WORTHY

In kindergarten and first grade, our little girl is
learning in many new and varied ways. She is
developing competencies. She can now play with
others; she is learning skills of communication such
as reading and writing. Other skills are being practiced, such as skipping, jumping, shouting, making
noise, and physically experiencing her sense of
power. Enthusiasm for life and learning are her

expressions of her worth. She knows what she wants, which is the same as having a value structure. When her values are derived from the beliefs of others, and expressed as "oughts" and "shoulds," they are inculcated values. Her own true value system is deeply entrenched in the core of her individual desires. As she goes to school, she individuates further into who she is.

Or she has been hampered, shaped, molded, and restricted into the box of inadequacy. Her identity, even at this early age, can be fixated in her safe choice of invisibility. Well-meaning parents may have already scripted her to a limited existence based on her being a girl, making sure her behavior is "appropriate" to their standards. She may have frozen her feelings by this time, following a stoic response to her world. Or she may begin a process of survival through competition, needing to win and hating to lose.

STAGE 5 — SELF-RELIANT

The elementary school years bring the possibilities of achievement. This is the stage in which friendships with other girls are important. A girl's capacity for concern is beginning to blossom. She is learning to make emotional connections. Success in the world of relationships is assured through giving and receiving friendship. Competence and confidence in skills – verbal, written, relational – are qualities of this stage.

Negatively, this self-reliance stage may reveal that she cannot make productive friendships. Strict parents may control her friendship choices. She is not learning how to be comfortably natural as a friend to other girls. Nor is she learning how to express her vibrant nature through her relationships with other non-family adults. She compensates for her failures by giving herself away or by "going it alone." When she gives herself away, she is symbiotically reactive to and dependent on those around her for her direction. Or she decides she cannot trust anyone and must rely on herself alone. Moving toward or away from others seems to be her only choice.

STAGE 6 — SELF-CONTRIBUTING

The adolescent years for our growing woman are the ones when she becomes comfortable with commitment. Her commitment to a boyfriend or a cause in the idealism of her teen years is her statement of separation from her family of origin, the original constellation of people who cared for her. Her mother and father or other childhood caretakers are left behind as she grows up. She arrives at her early adulthood with the capability of intimacy. The accumulative effect of her healthy upbringing was building in the years before her pubescence. Comfortable with herself in three areas – sexual, sensual, and spiritual – the adolescent girl, at approximately twelve years of age, has an emotional flow of self-acceptance. She uses her power to contribute to the world through loyalty in relationships and her genuineness in caring.

In contrast, the young adult woman can, instead, show serious inability to build loving relationships. The negative nurturing from earlier stages has accumulated. She may be limited in her capabilities for relating to others, male or female. She may not have the ability to separate, in a healthy way, from her family of origin. Her anxiety over her body or other perceived inadequacies contributes to harmful unhappiness.

STAGE 7 — SELF-CREATING

In this early adulthood stage of talent development, the budding Possible Woman is ready to create her life. She can plan and she can love. Her story is hers to author. Her joy and serenity are structurally in place to help her cope with any eventuality. She has an interest in others and is a healing presence.

Her negative counterpart may have an underlying depressive cloud resulting in addictions or compulsions. A growing sense of hopelessness pervades her very life. She will need some growth process, such as good therapy, to help her overcome the drain on her energy.

These seven stages happen to a little zygote-fetus-infant-girl as she advances toward her twenty-first year of life. The seven stages then recycle many times and are refined as one individual Possible Woman continues the journey of her total life cycle.

Our growth is never-ending, but consistently pushing to climb in a spiral of continual life expansion. For each woman, in her body, in her mind, in her emotions, and in her spirit, the spiral can be ever-heightening and ever-broadening. Or a woman can get stuck in the cages of her perceptions, an example of which might be her limiting herself to existing only as a physical body and spending her time, energy, and money trying to keep herself from aging or dying.

SELF RE-PARENTING

But what if you don't emerge from these stages with positive outcomes? What can you do? Women I've worked with have used a variety of techniques to heal the pain from various stages. One technique I have found especially useful in thirty years of working with women is Self Re-Parenting. This is a crucial concept. Each woman as an individual can be a support system unto herself. Any woman can re-parent herself.

My friend and teacher, Muriel James, expressed this theory of Self Re-Parenting in her book, *It's Never Too Late to Be Happy: The Psychology of Self Re-Parenting*. Through her help, I faced my own internal parent, who had treated me in very much the same judgmental manner that my father had. I began to take charge of this internal parent, making changes that amounted to mind taming. I worked diligently, developing a supportive, nurturing internal parent inside my own mind. That internal parent can now give me much of what I need. Self Re-Parenting is an ongoing process. Healing the negative chatter in my mind is a daily growth task. Even today, I can lapse into an attack of severe self-criticism. I use mind taming to acknowledge the attack and resist falling into the trap of believing my father's criticisms. Then I construct helpful thoughts to replace the old voice and its criticisms, and I forgive myself.

People who become parents get vital assistance in their own self-growth when they rear their children. As a baby progresses through each stage of development, the grown-up parents have the opportunity to heal the woundings of their own childhoods. If you are a mother or father, pay attention to the stages of your child's growth that give you trouble. In all probability, that same stage was one in which your parents failed you, so you get to do "double duty." If you can recognize the voice within you that needs to change, you can heal the child within yourself as well as parent and heal the child you brought into the world. You'll find it helpful to study good parenting techniques and the latest theories of positive child development. One book I especially recommend is *Giving the Love That Heals* by Harville Hendrix and Helen Hunt.

If we, as women, can begin to view ourselves as

flowers to be nurtured and tended, then we will do ourselves the great favor of re-parenting the wounded child of our past. Giving to others what you need for yourself helps you learn how to parent yourself. It is really true: what we give, we get.

From the plant kingdom, we learn about growth. Just as flowers need very little pruning, people need very little self-condemnation. Flowers need to be given water, air, good soil, sunlight, and time to grow. So do people. Without adequate water, air, soil, and light, flowers don't thrive.

A metaphor for humans comes from the plant world. Good soil is necessary for a seed to grow. The seed is the essence of each human being, and the soil is the individual's support – her or his environment and relationships. A container of soil represents the culture into which the individual human being is born. The seed that is planted, like human seedlings, will resemble its family. For the little human seedling, learning is like air. Air rich with oxygen helps the plant to come to life. The flow of emotions, laughter and tears, is the moisture provoking the growth for a human being. Moisture is the necessary ingredient for the seed to thrive into its true possible self. In humans, sunlight is the metaphor for work, and work is the contribution to the world – the light one human being can bring to its culture. Sunlight brings the crucible of stretching toward maturity.

Just as a gardener helps plants grow by giving tender loving care, so we humans can help each other grow by extending to one another the human equivalents of soil, air, water, and sunlight.

My husband Paul has a new profession – he has become a play therapist for children. His work with children aged three to eleven provides clear examples of self parenting. Paul's young clients learn to self-soothe and to be self-responsible and self-directing. He gives these children the opportunity to have a relationship with someone who is not judging, evaluating, teaching, molding, or shaping. Instead, he sees children as beings to be unfolded. This is brought about through the art of his relationship with them.

ON STAGE

One single individual life, with its stages, is a drama enacted in various locations. My therapy with women is concerned with helping them claim ownership of their own stage rather than being drawn onto someone else's stage as a character in someone else's drama. This is very difficult. Women have been programmed since childhood to be symbiotic and co-dependent, so they wait for someone else to assign them a role. To be autonomous, self-directing, and inter-dependent is the therapeutic task for women today.

We are on a new stage. As we enter the next century, women increasingly are included in the broad spectrum of world events. Leadership, ownership, and participation are emerging for women. The drama of one woman's life includes many possibilities. She can create the life of a fully functioning professional as well as mother her children. She can choose to be a wife or mother. She is able to be a single parent. She can have wealth in her own right. She can own and run a business. She is able to hold management positions in large corporations. She is ready to be of equal value to all human beings.

Review your life and its stages. Think of memories from infancy, toddlerhood, pre-school play age, elementary school, teen years, early adulthood, mid-life, and wise elder stages. Those stages you have yet to reach can be "remembered" in future desire form. Find pictures from each of these stages. Notice the systems of support around you. Declare yourself to be worthy of hope, will, purpose, competence, love, caring, and wisdom. Accept from others their positive response. If criticism is offered, sift out the helpful information, and discard the rest. This is called love of self. Love of self is essential for the Possible Woman.

CHAPTER SIX

WAGES

- *Did you get a raise?*
- *How much are you worth?*

oney and fair payment for services are consistent, major issues for women. Earning, saving, shopping, spending, and the world of money are issues that affect all human beings.

I was eleven years old when I began to drive the tractor on our farm. This was my first job; I was thrilled to receive fifty cents per day for plowing the sudan grass field. My father was my employer. He did me a very great honor when he sent a strong message about qualities of being, doing, and having. First, he trusted me to drive his valued Farmall tractor. (I was secure in my skill, even though he yelled at me many times for my mistakes. The underlying implication to me was that I was needed.) I was treated as one of the grown-ups, and even though that meant I was one of the "hired

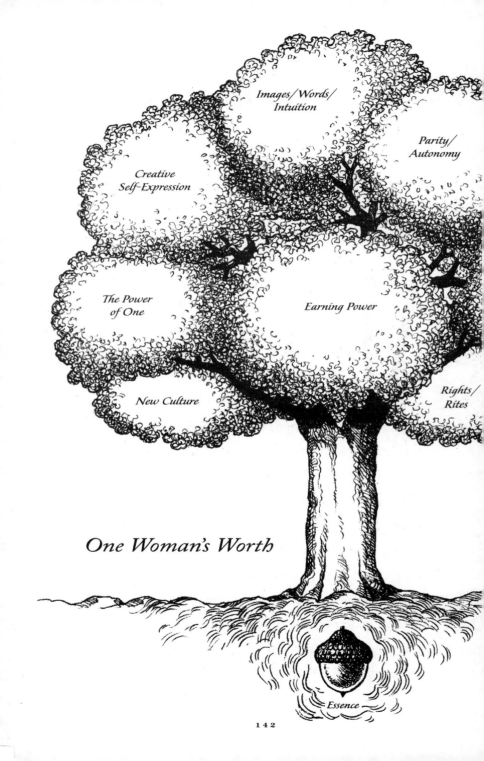

Images/Words/
Intuition

Parity/
Autonomy

Creative
Self-Expression

The Power
of One

Earning Power

Rights/
Rites

New Culture

One Woman's Worth

Essence

help," I felt accepted and valued and felt I belonged in his world. I had a sense of *being*. Second, he made a very straightforward bargain with me. He offered the contract, believing that I could do the job, and I accepted. He paid the wage with an air of pride in my having earned it. Money was an objective way to salute my *doing* a task. Third, he taught me to add and subtract and keep records of what I earned and what I spent. He never advised me on how I was to spend my money – I had total freedom of choice. I discovered the joy of *having* a few dollars earned by me, for me, and spent by me. On my father's farm, I was not discriminated against as a female. While it may have appeared to be an exploitation of child labor, I believed I was worth as much as the other farm hands.

Peace with the Past

I am still emotionally charged today when I earn money. Having the money is not where my excitement derives; it is in the purchasing power I get from spending the money. I learned that *being* comes first, then *doing*, and then *having*. I felt worthy, I knew I could achieve, and I would have the fruits of my labors.

THE MEANING OF WAGES

Interesting word, "wages." We speak of making a "living wage." In America, our minimum wage seems generous when compared with the earnings of people in many developing countries. In my childhood, to "work for wages" meant a farmer had not made a crop and was shamefully forced to find a wage-earning job to feed his family. The "wages of sin is death" brought an ominous meaning to the word, and the fear attached to "waging war" on another nation meant some price was to be paid.

Wages means money. Money and fair payment for services are symptomatic of current cultural imbalances for minorities, especially women. Passing laws to enforce equal pay for equal work, while being one step, may not solve the underlying problem. (Taking an aspirin for a headache may stop the pain, but the aspirin doesn't address the root cause of the headache.)

The root cause of this problem of equity in wages is connected to the human journey to date. A systems approach to the problem of equity in wages would suggest that as goes the system, so the individuals within the system are affected. Stock market fluctuations become like war room briefings that show who's winning and losing. In international commerce, some country or other is declared the winner in the economic war.

Whole systems thinking says we are interconnected. On the national as well as the local level, we are connected monetarily. When one part of the system is out of balance, the whole system suffers. Whether it be our natural environment, our pay scales, our workloads, our emotional support commitments, or the selection, promotion, and development of talent on the job, we are interconnected. Many ethical issues are involved.

Woman's earning power is a present and future challenge for our society. To adequately address the challenge is not easy without seeming anti-male or making women look like victims. But the fact remains that women do not receive equal pay for equal work in the United States of America, despite this country's global reputation for wealth and power. No single man alone caused the imbalance, yet individual male business leaders must bear the burden of initiating change. Change is needed, and change is coming.

SELF-WORTH

The Possible Woman is worthy, can achieve, and is ready to be paid for her efforts. When a woman works from a base of her worth as a person and her skills as a worker, the wages ought to follow. Those women who have made it through the metaphorical glass ceiling share the common characteristic of high self-esteem, leading to the conclusion that when a woman expects to be paid, the wages will follow her expectation. High self-worth and equal pay go together. Many women in leadership positions today want to help other women, and they are in position to support those to follow. The majority of climbers on the corporate ladder, however, are still men – not women.

Entrepreneurship is one (perhaps the best) path for women to reach earning power in accord with their worth. Statistically, the majority of new business owners are women. Motivation for women to start their own companies often surfaces when they become disenchanted with opportunities for advancement. In the business world, women have every right to reach for the brass ring of prosperity, and many are claiming that right.

ANOTHER MEANING OF WAGES

In my forties decade, I worked for a salary in a community agency. I wanted to make a change, but the risk of leaving a secure salary was monumental to me. Our family depended on my contribution to our operating income. I found the next use of the "wages" word. I bet on myself. I wagered our family comfort on my risk of entering private practice and becoming my own boss. I met the anxiety of this big change by going to my banker friend and negotiating a professional line of credit, thereby guaranteeing that I could contribute my share of the family finances. The line of credit meant that I could borrow the amount of my salary any month that my private practice income didn't suffice. The miracle for me was that I never had to borrow, and my income tripled within the first quarter of my first year as an entrepreneur. Friends helped by sending me clients and joined me as we attended classes to improve our professional skills. LaNelle

Ford and Joyce Spindle were good friends of the long road. We became partners in risk-taking as we entered our new businesses. We were, in truth, a network of support for each other. All three of us earned doctoral degrees, and all have been successful.

Networking is a familiar term in business circles today. Women "network" when they make contacts with others, receiving support, information about opportunities, and inspiration to make changes. Networking is similar to community relationships that thrived in the pioneer days. Barn raisings, quilting bees, and box suppers were informal social gatherings held in high good spirits – neighbors helping neighbors, friends helping friends, women helping women. Men in commerce and business have been networking for eons. From loyalties formed in male friendships, men guarantee their business success.

Networking is a powerful source of assistance to women in their quest for equity. To tap this source demands that women embrace concepts of loyalty. Networking, at its best, can replace destructive negative competition with other females with a sense of support, loyalty, and even good friendships.

WOMAN'S WORTH

We cannot depend on the past generations for help in determining women's worth in monetary terms. Before money was used as a medium of exchange, goods and services were traded in interconnected, bartering, networking societies. In hunter-gatherer and agrarian times, all labor had value even though the division of labor was often based on gender. On our farm, my father learned to quilt and taught me how to add and subtract, and my mother stacked feed and picked cotton – they shared life in equal partnership. But many marriage partnerships are far from equal, and 20th century society tends to value paid work over unpaid work and monetary support over nurturance or emotional support.

The decades since Rosie the Riveter earned her World War II wages have resulted in equal work but have not brought equal pay. The United States Congress has brought parity issues to the legislative table in the years since 1945. Legislation has not, and probably will not, provide the answer.

Certain changes are inevitable. One change on the horizon is that the post World War II managers and owners of the world of commerce – mostly men – are now retiring and dying off. Women in middle management are realizing the possibility of assuming corporate leadership. Women who spent the transition years as entrepreneurs and owners of small businesses are ready and able to fulfill managerial roles.

STRESS AND CHANGING TIMES

Understandably, all this change brings stress, and stress for both men and women is one outcome of diversity in the economic world. Changes in social structure are disturbing to any society because predictable role definition is outmoded and replaced with the uncertainty of change. Survival requires resilience. Coping becomes important, and resilience is the key to coping. Learning to "go with the flow" is a maxim of stress management. Resilience includes the ability to flow with the impact of new ways of being in the world. Diversity includes the concept of resilience. The glass slipper symbolizes the paradoxical desire for change with a simultaneous resistance to change on the part of women.

GLASS SLIPPERS AND CEILINGS

Transparent glass, made from sand, has meaning for the Possible Woman. Sand is of the Earth. Woman is connected to nature and to the Earth. Glass ceilings and glass slippers provoke thoughts about the paradigm shift in consciousness that grips our existence as women on this planet in this time. When Cinderella gave up the glass slipper in her haste to leave the ball before midnight, something was metaphorically foretold. The glass slipper, which brought her the Prince Charming with whom she purportedly "lived happily ever after" became the glass ceiling that holds back modern day Cinderellas in their quest for equality in the workplace. The fairy tale embodies the old paradigm. The glass slipper fit Cinderella perfectly, so there was no need to break it.

Some women I meet wear the slipper, marry the prince, and want to own the castle. When they realize they've lost themselves in the process of attaining "happily ever after," they want to leave the castle to find themselves, often in the world of business. As their self-search progresses, they want the prince to remove the glass ceiling in the workplace without giving up their glass slippers, their castles, or their places in the kingdom. In a remnant of the old story, these Cinderellas (perhaps unconsciously) expect the prince to rescue them. This expectation cancels out their stated desires for parity and equal value. As long as a man is responsible for her welfare, Cinderella is dependent, and she's exploiting the prince. She must find her own inner prince.

I have met with women who call their husbands' income "our income" and their income "my income." I find it impossible to be dependent on men and at the same time blame men for the plight of women and their wages. Being a victim is not a path to breaking through the glass ceiling.

In my twenties, I was busy bearing babies and working between pregnancies. My Cinderella dream was that my husband would some day earn $500 per month! Happiness for us was four children and his earning a decent salary so that we could afford a home and I could be the primary homemaker. The castle and all its furnishings depended upon his earning power. Our dreams and my dependence on my first husband ended with his death. Part of my grief involved the shock of realizing the plight of men as "breadwinners." In a life change that shook me like an earthquake, I discovered how it feels to be responsible for the care and feeding of four other people. Finding a new prince seemed a sensible solution – I knew I wanted to be married again and that I did not want to raise four children alone. I wanted companionship, and I wanted to share parenting responsibilities with another human being. Paul Barlow became my new prince/husband, and we created, as best we could, a "happily ever after" life. The magic we found was that of our own ingenuity, creativity, hard work, and perseverance. We kept at it. We didn't give up.

I still had growing up to do concerning money and responsibility. Thinking back, I discovered some things about myself. I looked at my Cinderella tendencies and my concepts about work and money. In my first job on the farm, I served an internship as a tractor driver. I suspect I was paid more than I was worth because I was still "in training." I was exercising my stages of development (self-starting, self-responsible, self-directing, and self-reliant). My self-worth depended on whether or not my father was pleased with my performance.

When I went to college, I earned twenty cents

per hour working in the business office, typing and filing clerical records. (Everything is relative – back then $200 per month was a good salary and bread was a dime a loaf. Today, that job probably would pay minimum wage.) For the first time, I had money to buy Christmas presents for my family. I had achieved a feeling of self-contributing.

Thirty years later, when I went into business for myself, my earnings exceeded six figures and were satisfying to my need for mastery and industry. My sense of being self-creating grew stronger as my psychotherapy practice grew and with every new educational program I designed, marketed, and sold. Talent, ability, skills, and motivation go into the mix of how much I get paid. I can remember the pleasure I experienced when I was offered my first consulting job with a small corporation. When I set my fee, friends insisted that I charge a fair market price. I appreciate the mentoring I received from both men and women who helped me set my expectations for pay commensurate with my training and experience. I learned, with their help, what other people charge for similar services. Expectations based on my self-image are also part of the mix.

I still get that feeling of satisfaction when I can buy material possessions with the money I generate. There is sharp contrast in my feeling and the feeling I observed my father express. I think my father valued his possessions, especially his money, and that he valued dollars in the bank more than the material goods he could buy with those dollars. It was as if he could one day *have* enough money, he could then *do* something, and from that he would *be* somebody. To me, being is basic; doing follows as an outsource of being, and the possessions I have acquired come from that wellspring of self-worth. One's point of view is the determining factor.

Shopping, spending, earning, and saving are bound up in decision making. If a girl child has made decisions from her infancy onward, she can make good decisions as an adult concerning money. If her childhood decision making process was externally controlled, she may have trouble when she shops and spends and with what she earns. Paychecks, savings accounts, pension plans, and wages may be more connected to self-worth than we think.

BELIEFS AND THOUGHTS

In the stages of my life, I have come to realize certain rules of behavior: As we think, so we become. As goes our perception, so becomes our reality. Fear will cause what is feared to be manifested. What we resist, persists. Thoughts create. Mental processes bring about material change. (Witness the redness of embarrassment in someone's face. Nothing has changed in the outside world, but veins, arteries, and capillaries send a gush of redness in response to a thought.) What we think about comes about.

Wisdom is wealth, and if I want to pass through my so-called glass ceiling, then I must stop thinking about the glass ceiling and start thinking about the world I really want.

Simply stated, this means to speak and think about what you do want, not about what you don't want. Create a positive vision. (To dwell on what is not wanted and decry that terrible thing, whether it be depression, victimization, unfair payment for services, or the plight of children in a third world country, does not solve the problem.)

Give yourself one hour to write a positive vision of your world. First, make sure your body is comfortable and your writing materials are at hand. Place your non-dominant hand on a blank page and trace around your fingers so that you have an outline of your hand, its four fingers, thumb, and palm. Label your little finger PAST, your next (fourth) finger, PROFESSIONAL, the middle finger, PERSONAL, your index finger, PHYSICAL, and your thumb, POTENTIAL. Your palm is labeled, PEOPLE.

Next, using your drawing as a visual cue, think about each of these aspects of your life:

1. Review your past.

2. Look at your professional training, your jobs, and career choices.

3. Remember all your personal involvements and your current intimate relationship commitments.

4. Assess your physical health.

5. Optimistically imagine your potential in all these areas of your life.

6. List the people who support you.

On another page, write a vision for your

future. Disregard any doubts or rational resistance. Dream in the most preposterously positive manner you can muster. Include your desires for professional, personal, and physical accomplishments. Ask for what you really want and write it without evaluation. This is the path for change of any kind and uses the power of the thought process to bring about what you really want rather than simply reacting to what happens. (We have good evidence that this is the way new businesses are created.)

WAGES AND SUCCESS

The formula for success discussed in "Rages" is appropriate for the important subject of wages. You'll recall that the formula for success is expressed mathematically as:

$$\text{Success} = \frac{SC \times SS + (G+E)}{(T+E)}$$

Success comes when Self-Concept is multiplied by Support added to Goals and Expectations and divided by the management of Time and Energy. Regarding wages, here's how it works: Your Self-Concept determines you will be paid about what you expect to be paid. Our worth begins inside, not outside. We need Support while we learn not to be dependent. The Goals we set are always tempered by our basic expectations, which are based on our beliefs about ourselves. So what is your time worth? What is your energy worth? Just how much are your efforts worth?

Although it's important to set goals that are realistically based on the current market forces, don't neglect to assign value to all those skills you have perfected as a woman in your culture. Managerial skills coupled with patience and perseverance and the ability to do many things at the same time are what women have practiced throughout the ages. Added to these practical skills, woman has the ability to introspect, to see the whole picture, and to communicate. These are worthwhile, viable, valuable skills.

What would you do if you received a financial windfall? Pretend you won the lottery and now you are faced with managing and spending several million dollars. Choose a sum equal to one million dollars for each year you have worked for pay. For example, I have worked since I was eleven, so my sum would be fifty-nine million. You will learn about yourself as you list the things you will buy, the people you will help, the business you will build, and the travel you can do. Your desires, needs, and values will be revealed. This exercise helps you set your goals.

The Possible Woman is a new model. She has never been here before. We are creating her as we go along. Just as pioneer women shouldered the loads of their day, we can rise to the occasion and create prosperity in our success as trailblazers and pioneers. We can take our rightful place in the ongoing evolution of the human species on this planet Earth. In doing so, we are ready to experience the freedom to become all we can be. When women are released to join in equal earnings for equal work, men are released from the burden of providing complete financial support, allowing both the opportunity to become more spontaneously alive. This is the wisdom of wealth for women.

CHAPTER SEVEN

SAGES

*Woman's wisdom is ageless,
timeless, and increasingly
available.*

W omen's wisdom is an elusive concept in present day mainstream ideology. Our culture seems to emphasize and value so-called masculine traits of aggression, competitiveness, rational thought, objectivity, and linear thinking. Wisdom often is associated with these traits. Women's wisdom has other associations.

In the 19th century, between the days of Jane Austen and Edith Wharton, a woman appeared to be wise if she was fragile, passive, submissive, and dependent on her male protectors. Today, feminism, the media, and political (often religious) voices do not agree on what identifies a wise woman. There is, however, a basic common thread.

Women have a deep instinctive drive toward life. Life energy is connected with survival. The

What will you be?

Intuitive

Ingenious

Loyal

Joyful

Powerful

Reverent of Life

Born of the Earth

Essence Realized

nature of one woman's body holds her unique drive
to foster life, to nurture, and to heal. Since, as
females, we can hold an embryo in our uterus,
give birth, and lactate milk for a human
infant, we have the genetic possibility of a drive to aliveness.

We are the products of the
blood mysteries with maid-
en, mother, and crone –
the patterns brought
from our ancient his-
tory. Every woman's
story includes her
menarche. Every
woman, young
and old, can
recall her first
period. How
that life passage
was treated
often affects the
underlying story
of a woman's
journey through
her emotional

life. Our emotional stories are the underpinning of our wisdom. From our emotional stories, we grow our sagacity. Your story, then, is the source of your wisdom as a woman.

Rites of passage for women in the last century were ignored or poorly regarded, with overtones of embarrassment and shame. We lost our rights and our rites. Consequently, we came to doubt our wisdom and even ourselves.

The reduction of the importance of birth and the invisibility of women's bodily functions correspond to our treatment of Mother Earth. The phenomenon of denial of our natural processes is connected to the habits and patterns of our modern, technological, mechanical, low-touch age.

When I was young, machinery was more important than my developing maidenhood. The purchase of a new car was a greater emotional event than my menarche. I was given more attention when I learned to drive the machinery on the farm than when I came into womanhood. Ironically, I became a good driver of cars, tractors, cream separators, and other heavy equipment. I find it somewhat comical that my worst fault is my "drive" that often "steamrolls" those around me.

I am, by training, a driver, but I learned the spiritual transformations of the three major woman stages without formal recognition or teaching. Out of my own craving for such ritual, I have created my own women's rites of passage. Some of these are described in the Possible Woman Workshop in Appendix A of this book. They are mini-dramas designed to mark a passage and are meant to help with the flow of transformation.

Realization of change sometimes needs deepening to all levels of the mind. I recall Sally, who had had a hysterectomy. This had provoked early menopause, and she was experiencing intense hot flashes and other physical symptoms. We co-designed her rite of passage. She wrote a letter, which was her way of saying goodbye to her uterus and entering the next phase of her aging process. Sally's ritual also acknowledged her pain over losing her ability to be a mother. Her goodbye, read aloud, was tearful and touching. She wondered what had been done with her uterus after the surgeon removed it and expressed her anger at being treated mechanically, without consideration of what the operation meant to her personally. She held a virtual funeral for the tissue taken from her body. In mourning her losses, she was released to celebrate the next stage of her womanhood.

Other rituals might be termed celebrations, for they are more about gain than loss. I remember the day Joan brought crackers and cheese to her therapy session, joyous over a promotion and pay raise. She had been promoted to field superintendent in an oil company after many years as receptionist and administrative assistant. The owner had been innovative in his decision — he told Joan she had been doing the job without the title for many years and that now he was giving her the salary and title to match the job she had been doing. She finally had received recognition for her skills.

Such a turning point in her life deserved formal attention, so we created a ritual on the spot. First, Joan listed all that her promotion meant to her. Second, she recalled what she had gone through in her years with the company. Third, she spoke of deserving the reward. We made her a certificate of recognition. I formally presented the certificate and, in a sober moment with tears in her eyes, Joan accepted it.

Our treatment of each other and our treatment of life here on this planet is often superficial, unaware, and not serious. We think in shallow ways about the flow of life. Ritual aids us in deepening our thinking about that flow. Our heartless covering of the Earth with asphalt, our depletion of her resources, and our disregard of the importance of our waste has been done with the same lack of care. Mother Earth seems to have the same longing for recognition and a return to respect for her body as do women.

THE FEMININE SPIRIT

The feminine spirit, originating in the body as a flow of emotion, reaching the psychological realm for both men and women and the spiritual realm for all, is dedicated to uniquely feminine qualities. These are qualities of the heart, of life, and of the energy of the life force. Feminine qualities are evolutionary in that they represent life-giving, life-sustaining, and life-development toward spiritual wisdom. The wisdom reveals itself through relationships and is refined in the crucible of each intimate relationship.

Wholeness for one individual brings to mind the full spectrum of color in one rainbow. Rainbows are a natural phenomenon, ageless and timeless, that can be seen when certain weather conditions are met. They represent truth, beauty, and goodness, three qualities of human life which are available. The feminine spirit in each Possible Human, male or female, is a rainbow of colors waiting and ready to transform the world.

Rainbows also remind us of that which is ageless and timeless. The wonderful women of my childhood were angels in print dresses. They came when babies were born, they served food in times of distress and celebration. They were cheerful, reliable, beautiful, and colorful, never whining or demanding. They supplied zest, enthusiasm, and heart for our farming community during the Great Depression.

My mother, Ola Victoria Kiker McNeely Layfield, is an active nonagenarian. Born in 1904, she has lived almost one century in this age of mechanical accomplishment. She drove a horse and buggy and eventually learned to drive cars and farm equipment. She cooked on wood stoves; her meals were made from homegrown ingredients. She helped in the fields as well as with the killing and butchering of chickens, pigs, and cattle, and she kept our family clothed and clean without benefit of electricity. She earned a college degree after my brother and I reached adulthood. Her retirement from teaching means she has adequate income in these last years of life. Her retirement as a church musician is yet to come. She practices unconditional love.

Mother's spiritual wisdom holds the values of the wise woman – the sage. Her wisdom is evident in her behavior. She asserts herself when needed, without becoming attached to a certain outcome. She gives without keeping score in a sincere generosity of spirit. She practices non-judgment of self and others. She nurtures, encourages, creates, and intuitively senses the cycles and flow of life. She is welcome wherever she goes. Her health is good, her mind is clear, and she is still contributing to her world. Mother exemplifies the colorful rainbow of the feminine spirit.

ENERGY IN COLOR

We human beings are of the Earth with its earthy colors. Reds, browns, and rich soil hues are Earth colors, symbolic of our tribal roots. Each of us was born into a particular family, inheriting the roots of that family and the patterns of emotions, intellect, and behavior to imitate as we grow into adolescence and young adulthood. Red is the color that symbolizes girlhood and our connection to our family.

Orange signifies our creative and reproductive capacity. Just as a sunrise (or Earth-set, a more accurate term, since the Earth moves around the sun) brings its vivid oranges ushering in a new day, so we women, in the feminine spirit of the mothers, can conceive, gestate, and produce. The blush of ripened fruit, peach-orange-pink, is like the skin of a newborn baby with all the exciting promises of hope. The life force is vibrant and palpable when hope is experienced. In scripture (Romans 5:4) we learn that our suffering teaches us patience, from our patience we gain perseverance, and from perseverance we receive hope. It is the suffering, patience, and perseverance of creative women that gives hope to the coming age. What we perceive as suffering may be, instead, life's expansion into increasing complexity and novelty. We regain hope when the concept is reframed as one of growth rather than useless or tragic pain.

Bright sunshine is yellow, the color of clarity, with the metaphorical attribute of the power of the sun. The sun is integral to life. We are made up of photons, of light energy. Each of us is a package of compacted light energy. The power to express one's wisdom, to bring forth the possibilities of a new day and the awakening of that unique essence within, with its potential for light in all the levels of existence: these are the birthright of all women. A living Possible Woman appears in all her wisdom when that one woman claims the power and light of her own sun – not the reflected light of someone else.

Green represents the color of growth. Grass, trees, flowers, people, societies, worlds, and even universes, growing with the green of love, empathy, and compassion. The body location for green is the heart. The next century may become the century of the thinking heart – just as this century was the century of the brain. The heart path is full of wise possibilities. In the communication-information age, we are beginning to search out the path of empathy and the concept of a thinking heart.

Neural research is redefining our concept of the brain as the only organ used for thinking. Paul Pearsall's book, *The Heart's Code*, reveals the evidence for cellular memory and for the possibility of neurons actually located in the heart muscle. Pearsall tells the stories of organ transplant recipients. The new memories, dreams, and behaviors of people who have received heart transplants indicate strong evidence that the cells themselves hold memory.

The rich blues of sky and sea suggest inclusion and connection. Sky blue represents woman's ability to communicate and relate. The throat and airways are the body location of this communion-unity location, connecting the head to the body. It is here that woman finds her voice. The voice of woman can transmit outwardly as well as inwardly. She can speak to her experience, and she can invite unity through her connection to others. Woman can lead toward the wisdom of intraconnectedness on the inside and interconnectedness on the outside.

Indigo, the beautiful blue-violet, twilight shade, is associated with woman's intellect and her mysterious intelligence in the "third eye," the place of her extrasensory perception. This is also the physical site of our intellectual capabilities. Intuition is a mysterious talent that, when we learn to use it, will bring our creativity to new heights.

Intuition brings knowledge without analytical, left brain work and tunes into spiritual flow and the emotional heart-brain with its capacity for information outside the realm of logic.

Purple signifies a wise person, man or woman, in an integration of wholeness of Self. Purple is connected to spirituality. Purple is like the dazzling dark of gestation time. It is woman in her fullness, wise and intuitive, integrated, whole and brimming with possibilities. It pictures, symbolically, her connection to her personal conception of a higher power. Resting as an invisible crown above her head, it is her next evolution in the spiral of growth. The coming of woman into full flower and her passion of possibilities are what this book is all about. Spiritual wisdom is the culmination of a woman's quest. Ultimately, the body fades and the spirit is her infinite identity of Self.

Colors help us express truth and experience goodness.

What is your favorite color? Find colors that give you pleasure. Thumb through art books or magazines for ideas. Use these colors to create your environment. Paint a room. Buy a new scarf. Plant some flowers. See what changes color can bring to your life. Write your responses in your journal.

I HAD A DREAM

In November 1994, attending a seminar at Resurrection Center in Woodstock, Illinois, I dreamed about a new handshake that was to be initiated by women. The seminar, entitled "Entering the Mind of the Maker," was created and directed by Jean Houston. Her teaching involved our projecting ourselves into each of the subjects we were studying – Thomas Jefferson, Emily Dickinson, Helen Keller, William Shakespeare, and Wolfgang Mozart. I came to know Thomas Jefferson and the others in new ways once I became them.

We were completing our week with a profound process called the "Asclepion." We revisited a page from Greek history, returning to the stories of healing in the ancient town of Epidauraus, the home of Asclepias, the god of healing.

The use of stories and myths from Greek, Roman, Egyptian, and other traditions has been an extension of a classical education for me. In Jean Houston's work, we are provoked to stretch beyond our edges and to create possibilities beyond our local stories. It was at this healing Asclepion that I had this dream in these three scenes:

Scene One was about my husband and me. We were remodeling our home. In my dream, the stereo was too large to fit on the square black marble pedestal. We were propping it up with a round pipe, approximately four inches in diameter, so that we could play the music.

In Scene Two, some young people were attending a seminar, and they were demanding their money back. It seems they wanted to buy videotapes instead of attending the seminar.

Scene Three began in a neighborhood in which the houses were modest and middle class and the street was tree-lined. A woman was being told that there was to be a new handshake. Women were to initiate the handshake with men, and the women were to place butter in the palms of their hands before initiating the handshake. The woman in my dream was reluctant, even resistant, to the changed handshake. As if it were decreed from on high, the handshake was to be initiated and, like it or not, she had no choice. In the dream, I went across the street, to the right side, to a similar house, where I found the owner to be a man. I asked him if he would help with the new handshake, and he agreed. He then went across the street to meet the woman and she offered her hand. He accepted the handshake and was not offended by the butter in her palm.

What could this dream possibly mean? Jean Houston created a deep and powerful drama on the spot, engaging the whole group in the transformative journey she calls "Therapaia," a process of deepening mind-body-spirit in transformation to the potential of the individual. It is different from conventional therapy, different from analysis, and different from persuasion. Therapaia is more of an unfolding of the true selves of the participants. Participants are able to trust, allowing the flow of expression from their depths. No attempt is made to analyze, judge, or think for another person. The atmosphere is one of attention and warm, unconditional acceptance.

First, Jean asked for a stereo. A participant brought out a boom box. Placing the stereo on my knees, Jean asked what the pedestal meant to me and what the pipe meant. I replied that the pedestal, for me, represented a good education. My country school curriculum did not include the study of Shakespeare, Greek mythology, and other subjects offered in higher quality schools. So, from my dream, I knew I was speaking to the longing for the marble columns of learning and knowledge, which would be partial support for the music of my life. The squareness of the pedestal meant the world of "squares" in academia. The black marble represented the finest of resources.

The pipe, brought in my dream to support the stereo, seemed to me to be a metaphor for my own intuitive woman's wisdom, which comes from something other than left brain intellectual pursuit. I knew the pipe represented a pipeline to my primitive, peasant, earthy knowing, which comes to me from the depths of my spirit without assistance from reading or teachers. The music represented the joys of my life. (Music has been a prime source of pleasure for me. Our family gatherings always were centered around music with everyone included without judgment of their musical ability.) Jean then challenged the entire group to work in triads, exploring what, to them, was the meaning of their own music, pedestal, and pipe.

Scene Two unfolded as a message about our

"seminars" – we are educating young people in methods that no longer excite or challenge them. Sometimes education is stultifying and boring. The young people are seeking new ways to learn, suggested in the dream by the purchase of videotapes. Jean asked the director of the program to bring all the cash she had taken in payment for the seminar. Jean then instructed the group to come and "get their money back." They lined up to reach into the bowl for money, refunded so they could buy their "videotapes." They told me what their videotapes meant in the real world.

We spent a very long time with 150 thoughtful, brilliant people from all over the Earth, sharing their dreams of what we need to make a better world. They spoke of ecological responsibility to Mother Earth, of institutions changing for the good of the population, and of many new ideas for a repair and restoration of the planet Earth and her people. As representative "youth," we were addressing the longing to be engaged in the real world. We were brainstorming ideas to sustain and restore our spaceship.

Scene Three was a picture of what might happen when woman becomes fully partnered in our world. It spoke to the rise of the feminine, the coming together of both masculine and feminine, internally as well as externally. No longer can we, as women, wait for the men of our world to give that to us. We must take initiative and share the load. Therefore, we can use the substance represented by the butter in the dream to bring forth the release of men from their bondage as conquest-dominance rulers. For men to become fully human and fully alive, they require release from the burden of responsibility for all commerce and industry on this planet. Men, as well as women, can then claim so-called feminine characteristics. When the feminine characteristics of vulnerability, nurturance, compassion, and intuition are seen as valuable, both males and females will develop them. Women can invite them and open the door for that to happen. In my dream, the man on the right side of the street helped the woman take the step. I interpreted this part of the dream to mean the inner masculine within the female. She must change her interior to include a more willing masculine self. As the dream director, I told the woman she had no choice. The time is now to make the change.

We guided the group in the sacred marriage of

the masculine energy to the feminine energy within our own souls. We also reached out to each other in the new handshake. There was a connecting, a healing, and wholing of each person individually. The group became a cohesive tribe with a oneness of energy that made us far more than the sum of the individuals present. (Yes, we did shake hands with butter in our palms!)

If dreams came to us as letters from God, would we open our mail? I think my dream was a letter from God, telling me that as a woman I hold a special gift. I have the gift of my mammary glands, which are the hallmark of warm-bloodedness and the way we feed our young. My dream gave me a new message about my worth as a woman. I hold the possibility of nurturing for all – babies, husbands, brothers, fathers, sisters, mothers, myself, and the world of Gaia, the living Earth, in her mothering of the life force. We are representatives of God, capable of extending love. Woman wants to become her true High Self, expressing that Self emotionally, physically, intellectually, and spiritually. It is the most joyful way to live.

My dream came to be a precious guiding credo for me. The remodeling of our home signified the new model older person. More women are now living many years beyond menopause and can contribute their wisdom in more ways. The placement of the stereo on the pedestal and the pipe means that we, having achieved longevity, can bring in new music, new joy, through our intellect and our intuition. From that, I developed the idea of four joys: the joy of learning, the joy of working, the joy of playing, and the joy of loving.

Scene Two, for me, is a metaphor for our waking up to how we teach our young people. It's time the media responded to the longings and dreams of thoughtful people instead of giving us shallow sound bites and uncreative programming. (Paul and I watch *Teletubbies*, which makes us smile, and *The X Files*, which makes us think. Not much else holds our interest!)

The third scene of the dream opens the way for women to claim their rightful heritage with the evolutionary growth of responsibility for initiating a new way of connecting with our brothers. It also creates the individual male in new form. His feminine side becomes alive, active, and appreciated when he finds his joy in learning, working, playing, and loving.

Dreams often reflect our reality, and they also can, like letters from God, open up our possibilities. My hope for all women is that they claim their possibilities in a new and better future for the whole human race. With woman's participation in the entire spectrum of human endeavor, we will change the future and the change will be good.

In her book, *A Passion for the Possible*, Jean Houston says: "Western women are leading the way toward the rise of women around the world to full partnership with men in virtually the entire domain of human affairs. And as women are being equally empowered, men are being freed to discover that activities often seen as 'feminine' – feeling, nurturing, collaboration, celebration, relationships – are in fact the domain of all. Personally, I believe this to be the most important change in human history.

"The rich mind style of women, which has been gestating in the womb of preparatory time, lo, these many millennia is catching on, and with it comes a tremendous change in the way we do things.

"Women emphasize process more than product; their special gift is making things cohere, relate, grow. Through women's eyes, relationships are more important than final outcomes. The world within is as important as the world without. Governance, games, education, work, health, society itself are held to new standards that honor the fullness of who and what we can be. This is a tremendous change, and once it is in full flower, the world will have turned a corner."

Jean Houston's belief that we can mythologize rather than pathologize is one that I find true and very workable in my psychotherapy practice. We are living myths. Our stories are really all we have. No story is pathological – it may be tragic, it may be comical, but it is the human condition and therefore sacred. Any perceived weakness covers a strength trying to come out. The life force is in us, and like the life force in a seed, it tries to show up.

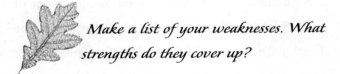

Make a list of your weaknesses. What strengths do they cover up?

WOMAN'S STORY TO WOMAN'S SOUL

My psychotherapy is aimed at helping clients shape their stories into forms they can accept. Successful psychotherapy creates one's personal story as a myth. The personal myth keeps the wisdom of the journey without reliving the pain of the journey in the here-and-now as an ongoing lament.

From one woman's story to the Soul of Woman in seven phases is my summary of the path of growth and development. I invite you, the women in my family, and all those adopted daughters and granddaughters who have entrusted their life stories to me to bring forth your story in its grandest form. I hope you will review your life and reveal yourself through your story, your spirit, your skills, your support, your script, your sight, and your soul.

YOUR STORY

From your family, your tribe, your story begins. You are needed, you are included, and you belong. You are an integral part of a system, never-ending, always unfolding another chapter as a member of your tribe, which is now the larger family of the Earth tribe. You can integrate what has gone before into your life and improve the flow for the good of all. The cages of the past are removed, your rage is transformed, and your place in the great story is assured.

YOUR SPIRIT

Your creative enthusiasm is held in your reproductive ability, unique unto you as the embodiment of the feminine spirit, with the energy to move mountains and create civilizations. In your spirituality-sexuality-sensuality lies the genius of what you are. You are free to create in your own artistic style whatever enhances the Earth and its people. No other being can do or be what you are equipped to do and be.

YOUR SKILLS

From your crafts, artistry, and skills, which may include weaving tissue in your womb, you know how to get things done. You can manage a family, a schoolroom, or the communications industry explosion. You can direct a choir, a band, an orchestra, a computer lab, political arenas, a corporation, a hospital, an alternative healing facility, a volunteer organization, a spiritual community, or a nation. You can answer any calling, and, in cooperation with others, you can contribute to the management of saving a whole planet.

Skills that are inborn plus skills you are building, your unique genius, can now come together in the most vital field of all: relationships. All our daughters are prepared in their blood to foster improved relationships. Our sons have the feminine energy to do the same. Receptivity and openness to new learning are the keys to change for men. Collaboration, cooperation, and communication are skills to be learned. Relationship skills are available from many sources. Books, television programs, counselors, and workshops abound. The joys of safe and loving relationships can be yours when you risk learning how to love.

YOUR SUPPORT

You may have found, through the hard work of growing, that giving support was a way of getting your needs met. By helping others meet their own needs, you found an identity, and you never had to know your own individual needs until that relationship gave you the jolt of separation. You have grown to recognize support systems from your environment and other relationships. You, as woman, now stand as equal partner to those friends or lovers who give and get support from you. You are free to network with other women. You are confidante, advisor, and strategist with your male brothers and friends as well as all other women. In the free-flow of your spirit, you stand equal to and side-by-side with other leaders, and you are cooperative when you are a follower. We are connected to all life and all life is connected to us. We have the right to be sustained and the responsibility for sustaining life. Being in the flow is the desired goal.

YOUR SCRIPT

You are free to write your own script for your life. You must do so, for, in truth, no one else can or will. Your talents are needed. Your mind map, mental model, learned drama of life, plus your own creation built on ever widening circles of awareness, give you the material for your life drama. The script of your unique life is created through the expression of your individual thoughts, your feelings, your behavior, and your beliefs. You are learning that your own beliefs and thoughts are like prayers sent into the atmosphere and that they become manifest.

YOUR SIGHT

Vision is many-layered. Sensate vision, with its mechanical practicality, sees only what can be measured or weighed. Vision from your heart can imagine better relationships and healing of bodies, even influencing machinery. Vision from the mind can create new structures in the physical world. Vision from your soul can bring the human race into the future path of altruism. Increased vision, widened horizons, and skills of deeper meditation can bring your "sight." You can trust your intuitive knowing. You can use your intellect to enhance and support your vision.

YOUR SOUL

As an eternal being, you can know you are infinite, while living a body experience. Given this view of yourself as a field of consciousness surrounding the physical organism, you can begin to reach for your possibilities. The connection of the thinking heart to the mighty brain is the next pathway for our scientific study. I think our hearts somehow hold the flow of the soul. Your own heart energy will connect you to all life. Your soul energy is blessed of God. As your shadow work leads you to the light, so your soul illumines the world you touch. As your heart pulses, your light radiates into the universe from the soul of you.

THESE THINGS I BELIEVE

The greatest resource on the planet Earth is the human being. The greatest development of that resource takes place in the area of human relationships. The best situation for development exists when the developing person is actively engaged in the development of another human being. These are the goal principles of the Positive Approach to Human Development, as stated by Dr. William E. Hall at the Nebraska Human Resources Foundation in the middle of this century, long before they were acceptable ideas. Paul Barlow was his student. He has lived the positive approach within our relationship and in all his connections with others.

I have also witnessed and been blessed by the Positive Approach as modeled by my mother. She never knew Dr. Hall, but she has lived the principles. I remember once telling my mother that I could never repay her for all she had done for me. I reviewed all the times she had helped in the most selfless manner throughout all my life, and most especially during those times when I was going through a dark night of the soul. Her reply to my attempted gratitude was, "You don't repay me. You pass it on to someone else."

One Possible Woman actively engages in the development of another woman, who actively engages in the development of another women, who mentors and encourages other women, until all women have been developed in the great web of life. We will then reach the critical mass that turns our world to the light.

For our world of women, and men, I hope that we advance these skills of relationship to an enlightened vision of a safe civilization. I hope we empower leaders who give us a new vision. The new vision must commit to the children, creating a world of safety for the next seven generations. I hope that our children and young people will once again feel the lure of becoming. I hope we will pledge to include our wise elders in our caretaking and appreciate their wisdom. Including elders in daily life adds a rich dimension now thrown away. I hope we will embrace our lesbian sisters and gay brothers with full acceptance of their genetic inheritance. I hope we will show ecological responsibility and friendliness. I hope we can manage our commerce and governance without war, torture, or other destruction. I hope that we can commune with all sentient beings, all life on the Earth, as servant leaders. I hope we become aware of the meaning of the loss of cultures and species. I hope we can join the galaxies with a shared sense of purpose, not just for our own Earth and its solar system but for the entire expansive universe. I hope we can become representatives of love, which is God.

Our shadow rises to meet us everywhere. The shadow is that dark, denied, unrecognized aspect of life held within us and projected onto the outer world. The shadow shows up in the events, behaviors, and people that we find undesirable or repulsive. The shadow is in the unconscious or unaware part of our consciousness, and it amounts to an out picturing of our dark side. The shadow is not to be denied, projected, or disowned. The good news about the shadow is that it can be the guide through which we find the path of our movement toward the light.

We evolve toward the light, and the light is the ultimate source. We are the extension of the great All in All, and the best expression of that force is love. When we learn how to love one another and express our love of all life in our actions, we will have our next breakthrough in the arena of human endeavor. The Possible Woman will have evolved into the Possible Human. We will then experience the Possible World, and, beyond that, the Possible Universe.

APPENDIX A

The Possible Woman Workshop

Since 1973, my work as a change agent in the lives of women has led me to create study groups, seminars, and workshops where women could detach from daily life for the purpose of self-awakening, to discover themselves as individuals. Come with me now through your imagination to one of these weekends. We will stay in a hotel on Padre Island off the Gulf Coast of Texas, and we will join together in a workshop called "The Possible Woman." We use many guiding textbooks. *The Possible Human, The Hero and the Goddess,* and *Life Force* by Jean Houston and *Goddesses in Everywoman* by Jean Shinoda Bolen are favorite resources.

The Greek, Roman, and Egyptian gods and goddesses were the beginnings of modern day psychology. Through the study of these myths, we see the psyche – the soul – in ourselves. Psychology really means "the study of the soul," and this is soul work. The soul seeks meaning and purpose. Through the story we live, we see the soul on its journey. Every woman lives her story. Our workshop is designed to help the story express her spontaneous aliveness.

In the workshop, we explore and recall all the various roles lived by women. We choose seven roles and seven goddesses in the Greek mythic tradition to portray those roles. The number seven is symbolic and meaningful. There are seven notes on a musical scale, seven colors in our rainbow, seven sacraments in religious traditions, seven candlesticks in the book of the Revelations, seven days in the week, and seven body energy centers called chakras.

The seven Greek goddesses gave a general description of the whole of one woman. Each of the goddesses reveals a picture of the many different personalities inside us. They are like our sub-selves, our characters on stage in the life drama we are living. They represent a few of the major roles we live in our play.

Come now, in your imagination, to the workshop and prepare to answer those all important questions: Who am I? Who could I be?

MOTHERS AND DAUGHTERS (DEMETER AND PERSEPHONE)

We first meet on Friday night. You are asked to remember yourself as your mother's daughter. We review the myth of Persephone, the little girl who walked with her mother, Demeter, through a meadow, reached down to pick a flower, and fell through a crack in the earth. She ended up in Hades, where she was raped. Her mother went crazy with fear and searched for her far and wide. She finally appealed to Zeus, the big male god, who arranged for Persephone's return. (The story has much more rich detail, but these are the key events in the life of mother and daughter.)

We try to understand how our own birth, babyhood, toddlerhood, and early childhood plays out the myth. One crucial turning point as women is that time of life when we leave our mothers and begin our journey as grownups. We also try on the role of the mother who anguished over the loss of her daughter. In exercises designed to provide holding and nurturing, we help each other with the memories and reflections of our own losses and journeys to our personal Hades. We explore leaving our mothers and the emotional hold our mothers have over us. We also examine the emotional energy flowing from us to our mothers. We do this with dancing, singing, acting, and storytelling. The separation of the daughter from the mother is acted in impromptu drama with music and lots of tears and laughter. Sometimes serious, sometimes raucous, sometimes playful, and sometimes through very hard emotional birthing, we become aware of ourselves as little daughters and big mothers.

Saturday morning, you are invited to walk on the beach, journal, meditate, or just rest. You might choose to join Marj Kutchinski and Gail Blanpied as they lead the group in tai chi just as the sun rises over the water. The solitude and the sense of being both alone and supported bring about a dawning self-awareness as the day dawns.

FATHERS AND DAUGHTERS (ATHENA)

After breakfast on Saturday morning, we meet as a group to talk about fathers and daughters. I get out my old talking stick, which is a limb pruned off an oak tree that grows near my office. This stick has served in many workshops and has heard the stories of hundreds of women.

We take turns in the women's circle, holding the talking stick. Holding the stick means that you have the floor, and you keep the floor – and the stick – as long as you wish to talk. We review the myth of Athena, the father's daughter. Each woman in the circle is free to talk or just to listen to stories about fathers or other male caretakers and childhood. The stories are poignant, touching, interesting, funny, and often very insightful. We act out the story of Athena, who was the child of Zeus and Mettis. She grew up inside her father because he swallowed her mother before she was born. We are amused by the metaphor of the patriarchy swallowing the matriarchy. At the workshop, we re-enact the drama of springing full-grown from the head of the father. Athena comes forth, complete with breastplate and armor and a mighty war whoop.

Each woman has her own unique play, a life drama based on her experience with her father or her fatherless condition. The outcome of the Athena-Zeus drama is that a woman born from her father's world is carried into larger realms of being. Her very DNA includes his masculine qualities.

Athena is an excellent prototype for women in equal

partnership with men. Just as Athena stood side by side with male gods and was goddess of crafts and wisdom, so the vision of that becomes a possibility for the Possible Woman. She can recognize her little girl dependencies. Her awareness of being caught in the prison of her father's patriarchal world may bring the suffering that attends birth. Many express their journey of realization of the patriarchal life as that of a comfortable, dependent little girl who, metaphorically, did grow up inside her father. Once recognized, the work of creating oneself can begin. Transformation may take a long time, or it may happen in a miraculous "holy instant."

The door of awareness opens, and there is no going back. The Possible Woman is recognized, and she begins the process of transformation into an independent woman balanced in both masculine and feminine traits. Her leadership, her wisdom, and her inventive creativity become possibilities for her real experience. The foundation is her realization of her equal value. Athena is the archetype, the pattern, for women's leadership development.

WIVES (HERA)

Saturday afternoon we enter and explore the role of the wife. The story of Hera becomes our script, and we find ourselves in that great lady consort role or in her dark self, the jealous bitch who can wipe out whole civilizations with her rages. Emphasis is on the positive elements of being a wife, being married, and on the individual woman's essence itself.

We study the four rungs of the ladder of love, a concept I use in counseling. The first rung is erotic love and its magnetic sexual attraction, which guarantees the survival of the species. The second rung of the ladder of love is the answer to the inevitable power struggle that all marriages create: agape love, which ensures the safety of the other rather than making war against the other. To climb to the third rung requires real commitment. When all threat or thought of divorce is ended, then this role becomes an integral sub-self (a self that can relate in a grownup way) for a thoughtful, conscious woman. She, as the wife, climbs to this third rung which is called *philea* – family love. To be family with one's husband means life-long commitment to growth. The fourth rung, at the top of the ladder, is altruistic love or charity, *caritas*. To live in charity with one's beloved is the ultimate for the wife role.

The role of wife is unlimited when marriage becomes a conscious creation – when two committed people dedicate themselves to a more mature marriage relationship with thoughtful, deliberate design. In this type of marriage, woman, as wife, is offered the opportunity to learn how to love instead of the limitation of only trying to get love.

In my practice, I have encountered many wonderful, intelligent women trapped in the mental model of trying to get love. A woman trying to get love seems to believe that she can only be happy when her man does what she wants, when he gives her love in a prescribed way. When she wants him to be a certain way, she is doomed to an outcome that depends on his obedience or rebellion. She is basing her happiness on how he ought to become, a picture that is of her own making. Instead, she could choose to change her internal model of expectation, engage in effective relationship therapy, or decide to give up, leave him, and move on.

I have worked for more than twenty years in the field of marital therapy. The great privilege of working with so many couples has been a liberal education for me. I believe that only in the marriage commitment and the crucible of day to day relationships do we heal our wounds and reach our potential. I say that because it is in marriage that we travel the path of the hero's journey, the journey that takes us repeatedly through the spiral of growth. We go to the underworld and learn our life lessons on the road of trials that are provoked by the partner we have chosen on this mystical journey of soulful marriage.

Imago Relationship Theory, as expressed by Harville Hendrix in *Getting the Love You Want* and *Keeping the Love You Find*, is the best method I have found for couples who want to learn more about how to love one another, but reading the books is not enough. Most couples need a coach to help them learn the skills that take them beyond the unaware, unconscious marriage. A marriage is unconscious when the partners behave in old patterns, most of which are limitations they adopted from their parents – they unconsciously foster a relationship that will not rise above the marriage they observed as children.

Simply stated, Imago theory holds that one's life partner is the provocateur of one's leftover unfinished business. Our childhood wounds always show up in an intimate, committed relationship. Since those wounds were begun in relationship, the healing comes through relationship. The healing requires learning skills beyond those learned in childhood. Marriage can be the crucible in which each partner is refined to the gold of the true self. Such is the value of a long-term conscious marriage relationship.

In the Possible Woman Workshop, we look at the wife role and resolve to return to our relationships with the commitment to transform every conflict into the next round of our growth and learning. Having a willing partner helps. One way to make your partner willing is to resolve to meet this challenge: interact with your spouse or anyone who is in relationship with you without blame, judgment, fault-finding, condemnation, criticism, or fixing. Listen empathically, validate them for the meaning of their communication, and re-frame every conflict into a cry for help. For indeed, if what they say or do is not loving, it is a cry for help. Here's an example:

Jim and Susan come to my office, seeking relief from their angry, depressed, and hopeless state of marriage.

Their first session begins with my coaching a new way of conversation. They learn to listen, reflect accurately on what was heard, and express understanding of the meaning of those words.

Susan says, "I was angry when you didn't come home on time. You do this all the time and I've asked you not to over and over."

Jim replies, "If I heard you correctly, you said you were angry when I didn't come home on time. And you said I do this all the time though you have asked me not to. Did I get it?"

Susan replies, "Yes."

Then Jim asks, "What else?"

Susan tells him, "That's it for now."

Jim makes a validating statement, " I can understand how you must have been hurt." Empathizing with her, he adds, "I can see how you feel. I can imagine you were really mad." He goes on listening until it's clear he understands what she said.

The technique provides him a safe way to respond to Susan's anger. And when Susan mirrors Jim's expression of understanding, she responds with sincere empathy. That's possible when someone feels heard and his or her feelings are validated.

INDEPENDENT WOMAN (ARTEMIS)

Later on Saturday we look at Artemis (Diana in the Roman tradition), the goddess of the hunt and the moon. Through Artemis, we discover our capacity to claim our own territory and to set goals. Metaphorically, we are aiming the silver bow and arrow described in the myth. Taking aim physically and learning to look at an object or goal creates a body ready to cooperate with a mind that is making new ideas of possibilities in three areas:

1. qualities of being,
2. accomplishments/achievements in the arena of doing, and

3. tangible, material things desired for having.

Imagine walking on the beach and dreaming of your desires, then sitting on the sand while you write in your journal lists of things you want. These lists become a wish list from which you can select possible goals. They are sorted into three lists, things you want to *be*, to *do*, and to *have*.

The wishes are the brainstorming of wants and desires. Our wish lists are like seeds. From these mounds of seeds can be selected goals to plant. All goals need to be drawn from individual wishes, desires, or wants. Many women's goals come from "oughts" and "shoulds" imposed by others or by society. The responsibility for changing this rests within, not with the world on the outside. As they say in Alcoholics Anonymous, "It's all an inside job." The changes, once made on the inside, become reality and materialize in the outside world. The goals become commitments. This portion of the workshop is helpful in stimulating our possibilities, taking aim, mobilizing support, and creating from the wellspring of our potential.

Artemis is the prototype for taking aim. She also was midwife to other women. We look at our friendships with women and the ways in which we can support and cooperate. Inclusion, involvement, inspiration, and intention rather than competition and comparison are the suggestions for developing this role.

Linda Wind is an example of the Artemis archetype. Linda and I met in the early 1980s when she was living in Corpus Christi, Texas. She helped me plan, market, and conduct workshops and seminars for women there, including one called "21st Century Possibilities for Women." They were the beginnings of the Possible Woman seminars, which continue today. Linda organized the first Possible Woman Cruise in 1997. Her aim is networking and leadership development for women. In her own style, she has masterminded the connections for hundreds of women who also reach for their own Possible Woman potential.

Linda's own story is typical of many women who have been in the corporate managerial world in this country. She was promoted to a national sales management position and discovered she was earning more money but enjoying it less. She began having health problems due to the strain of extensive traveling and long work hours that didn't give her time for a more balanced life. Juggling many endeavors, she earned her MBA degree during these stressful years and eventually decided to create a different work environment, one better suited to her needs. Linda applied principles of positive self-development in her new vision. She assessed her health, made changes in her life, and began to create a positive vision of her future.

SPIRITUAL WOMAN (HESTIA)

Saturday night we turn our thoughts to spirituality. The Divine Feminine recalls that part of woman's nature which is deeply spiritual. Though we are not addressing religion, we examine our inner beliefs about ourselves. We recognize that we have an invisible force that inhabits our mind-body field of being. We accept the spiritual nature of ourselves as women, represented by Hestia, the goddess of the hearth. A special formal dinner is served. We come to the dinner in solemn procession, all of us dressed in white. As the meal is eaten, conversations are lively, intimate, and animated. When we finish dinner, a ritual has been prepared with elements of the hero's journey.

Joseph Campbell wrote about this universal archetype, or pattern, in many cultures in *The Hero with a Thousand Faces*. It is a pattern often repeated. The hero – male or female – gets the call to adventure, either through external crisis or internal urgency. This pressure builds, almost like that of a butterfly emerging from a cocoon. Helpers may want to relieve the pressure, but the hero must cross the threshold, entering something new and unknown. Having crossed the threshold, the hero goes through the depths of the underworld birthing process, encountering all sorts of tests. The underworld journey amounts to a road of trials. Helpers again may appear, with the hero eventually reaching some sort of acceptance with the peace of surrender or atonement. Following that, a return to the outer world brings the hero again to a threshold, which has its own struggles for emergence. The gift from the learning is brought to the outer world and the cycle completes itself, followed by yet another call to adventure.

I have been privileged to watch many women travel this hero's journey. Sometimes, the call to adventure comes in the form of an inner voice, asking for something to fill a void in her boring life. The call also can come from cataclysmic outside events, such as hurricanes, serious illness, or abandonment.

One very common scenario is the woman whose husband divorces her after many years of marriage. She is thrust into the call to adventure through an act from the outside world over which she has no control. The struggle at the threshold is her attempt to get her husband to return to the marriage where she felt safe and protected. His refusal casts her into the underworld with the subsequent road of trials. She is aided on her fearful journey by helpful friends and/or therapists, who can midwife her transition. At some point in her underworld darkness, she begins to reach a new, sacred marriage within herself. In her awakening to wholeness, her inner male and female selves are joined. She discovers her masculine strength and her ability to make it alone. She often further discovers that she can make it *better* alone. The time comes when she can create her life independently. Then comes the struggle of leaving her support group or her helpful therapist, which amounts to a hero crossing the other threshold of her return to the outer world. She declares her independence of her therapist and returns to the outside world, fortified with new knowledge and power. She now possesses the elixir of healing. She is a new being with her own capability of helping others in similar circumstances.

Today, there is a new heroism, representing much more than the warrior-hero model. Women, now ready to join in full citizenship, bring into play a new potential for the planet Earth. The new model for both sexes includes cooperation, sensitivity, communication, and intimacy coupled with independence.

In a role playing event staged on Saturday night, our participants have the simulated experience of the hero's journey. First comes the call, which we announce at dinner. Suggesting to them that they came here expecting something, we give the invitation to enter into the joy of self-discovery. The mystery and the initiation to follow is the symbolic transformation to new possibilities. And so the call to adventure is issued.

Following the dinner meal, participants come, in quiet procession, to a threshold and guardians who ask them questions. The questions ("Who are you? What could you be?") evoke thoughtful answers from each woman about her mission in life. When a woman has answered, she crosses the threshold and enters a candlelit circle. Gail Blanpied is there with her Irish harp, playing beautiful meditative music. Gail leads a guided meditation in which you experience in imagery the successful completion of all that you want to be, do, and have.

The evening continues after a circle "go round" in which each woman, if she wishes, again holds the talking stick, and her words fill the sacred space. She is given some wood chips that symbolize her release and transformation from all that has constrained her in the past. Linda Savage has prepared a fire in a little hibachi, setting off the smoke alarm, which brings levity to the meeting. We take the fire to the balcony, and you cast your wood chips into it to transform, in this symbolic crucible, all your pain and past limitations. These are symbols of your road of trials in the hero's journey. We meet then in the sacred marriage, in which you come together with your own internal beloved of the soul, claiming the essence of yourself as an individual and your willingness to receive the boon of great blessing.

In a quiet, thoughtful, almost prayerful journey, we go to the ocean and cast into the water a handful of seeds. The casting of the seeds is our simple but eloquent symbol of the creative future and the possibilities of your one life as one Possible Woman. We stand at the ocean in a moment of quiet unity with each other and with all life.

In *The Hero and the Goddess*, a book about the voyages of Odysseus, Jean Houston tells in much detail about the mystery and initiation that can create a new story for any woman in her hero's journey. A great model for the Possible Woman, the goddess Athena is Odysseus' guide and strategist.

Our evening continues with skits, songs, riotous laughter, dance, and joyful celebration. Each weekend brings different creativity from the women who attend. Women from three generations of one family have been present on several occasions. The atmosphere of belonging, inclusion, and warm acceptance is inevitably healing and encouraging.

In the journey of the hero, we are preparing our return to the outer world and our internalization of what we have learned. Re-entry across another threshold – in this case, into the outer world of our families, our work, and our communities – is a part of the process. We are learning to bring the transformation we have experienced into the outer world of our lives.

Sexual-Sensual-Spiritual Woman (Aphrodite)

On Sunday morning, you can again walk on the beach, journal your thoughts, and experience tai chi. Later, the group convenes for the healing, wholing final session. We study the goddess, Aphrodite, and re-claim our full selves in one unified being. Aphrodite is the metaphor for the whole woman. She was both dependent and independent, and represents fullness of self. We are women with unique individuality, each of us sexual, sensual, and spiritual. We have now discovered we can be all three of those in one individual woman. We are indeed full, whole, and complete.

When the weekend is over, you have met yourself as the Possible Woman. Hopefully, you have been released to claim the essence of your being and from that, you can do what you find as a mission in life. Based on your beingness and your abilities, you will bring to your world and your life all the material possessions you desire to have. All of this – without guilt, shame, or fear. Is it possible? I believe so. I have seen it happen with many women in the last quarter of the 20th century.

Something changes for many women in the process of the workshop. The participants tell me they received permission and encouragement to continue the journey toward reaching their particular personal potential. They become more aware and more awake. They return to school, they make changes in their personal relationships, they reach for advancement in their careers, and they become of better service to the world. Because they are changed on the inside, they enact positive change in their outside world.

In studying and synthesizing myth and symbol from many traditions, women can claim the freedom of release from old expectations. The courage to make changes and to create a better, more productive life comes from the experience of the workshop. The seven traditional roles are not seven cages. They are part of our integrity as whole beings. They are like a board of directors in our own corporation. Each archetype is important. Bringing all seven into balance is the lifelong hero's journey for the Possible Woman.

These seven archetypes can become integrated into physical, mental, and spiritual practice. One woman who attended the workshop reports that she now has seven mountains she visualizes in her daily meditations, especially when she is faced with decisions to make. For my own version, I have discovered correspondence with the eastern system of chakras – the physical body's energy centers – and the colors of the rainbow. Red is the color for the root chakra with Persephone, the girl who comes from her particular tribe. Her chakra is at the base of the body and she is our uniquely feminine sexuality and our connection to our earthly tribal inheritance. Orange is for Demeter, the goddess of the reproductive organs and our creative mother potential. Yellow, which is symbolic of ethical use of power, is Artemis' color. Her position is in the power center of the body, the solar plexus. Green, the color of life and growth, is for Aphrodite, the goddess of love resting in the heart center. Blue is for Hera, the wife. Her domain is the connecting-communion passages of the throat and airways. Indigo or blue violet is the color for Athena, who resides in the brow, brain, and "third eye" of the forehead. She is our strategist and intuitive intellect at work, the trusted mastermind. Hestia completes the system with her place in the spiritual center or crown of the head, and her color is purple.

The Possible Woman Workshop is one effort made to engage the genius of woman in the full participation of life on the planet Earth. We are at an incredible juncture in the evolution of our species. Population, communication, and longevity are three explosive factors for our planet. All women are needed. The entry of more than half the human race into mainstream decision making will profoundly change the course of human events. To avail ourselves of the creative input from all the minds and all the souls who are affected by decisions made in our ecological structure is the only sensible path to follow. Inclusion of the feminine spirit and the power of the feminine holds hope for the restoration of Mother Earth, our feminine home.

APPENDIX B

List of Recommended Readings

CHAPTER 1 — AGES

• King Arthur's time through the eyes of the feminine:

  The Mists of Avalon by Marian Zimmer Bradley, 1982.

• A look at our ancestry with a liberal education in anthropology:

  Clan of the Cave Bear and other books in that series by Jean Auel.

• A thought-provoking look at a significant shift in our long buried past:

  When God Was a Woman by Merlin Stone, 1976.

• A new look at the agrarian age with sober possibilities unless we wake up:

  Ishmael: An Adventure of the Mind and Spirit by Daniel Quinn.

• How would your life be different? Questions that give dignity and worth to every girl child:

  A Circle of Stones, by Judith Duerk, 1999.

• A hilarious account of 17th and 18th century efforts to understand conception:

  The Ovary of Eve by Clara Pinto-Correia, 1997.

• A sometimes horrifying, sometimes funny book of actual quotations – things men have said about women:

  The "Natural Inferiority" of Women: Outrageous Pronouncements by Misguided Males compiled by Tama Starr, 1991.

CHAPTER 2 — CAGES

• More about Bolen's personal journey with discoveries about feminine stories:

Crossing to Avalon by Jean Shinoda Bolen.

• A story of awakening to consciousness for one woman who could no longer deny her true self:

The Dance of the Dissident Daughter by Sue Monk Kidd.

• An examination of American family life:

The Way We Never Were: American Families and the Nostalgia Trap by Stephanie Coontz, 1992.

• A helpful book for healing the pain when trust has been broken:

After the Affair by Janis Abrahms Spring, Ph.D., 1997.

• The true story of an unwanted Chinese daughter; heartrending story of a courageous woman who refused to be bound by her culture:

Falling Leaves by Adeline Yen Mah, 1997.

CHAPTER 3 — RAGES

• A book about how the New Testament is not a detriment to women's leadership development for any person who reveres scripture and fears that a desire for equality between the sexes is a violation of Christian principles:

What Paul Really Said about Women by John Temple Bristow, 1988.

• The writings of Elizabeth Cady Stanton and Susan B. Anthony, particularly *The History of Woman Suffrage.* When women could not vote, these two pioneers spoke and wrote powerful messages that paved the way for present-day inclusion of women in the political process.

• An experiential immersion into the lives of three great Americans – Emily Dickinson, Thomas Jefferson, and Helen Keller – and a good guide for breaking free and claiming personal possibilities:

Public Like a Frog by Jean Houston.

• A guide for defeating anxiety, insecurity, anger, and discouragement and making happiness the very purpose of life:

The Art of Happiness by His Holiness the Dalai Lama and Howard C. Cutler, M.D., 1998.

• Leaps of fear, faith, flying, and the art of falling – wisdom from the trapeze:

Learning to Fly by Sam Keen, 1999.

CHAPTER 4 — PAGES

• Necessary learning for any woman who wants to keep her body and mind healthy:

Women's Bodies, Women's Wisdom: Creating Physical and Emotional Health and Healing by Christiane Northrup, M.D., 1998.

• The transformative power of music is revealed in excellent manner by Don Campbell in all his books. These are favorites of mine: *Music and Miracles, The Mozart Effect, The Roar of Silence*, and *Music: Physician for Times to Come.*

• A must for any woman interested in personal power and healing – the alphabetical list of maladies and the psychological meaning of each is miraculously accurate:

You Can Heal Your Life by Louise Hay, 1984.

• Possibilities for shaping our own destiny as women, for the first time ever:

Empowering Women by Louise Hay, 1997.

• Good reading for developing mind, body, and spirit to your fullest potential:

How to Think Like Leonardo da Vinci: Seven Steps to Genius Every Day by Michael J. Gelb, 1998.

• Written for executive leadership re-invention, this book is a great revelation of where power lies – that our winning strategy may prove to be our limitation is an intriguing idea for self-awareness:

The Last Word on Power by Tracy Goss, 1996.

• For putting spirit into decorating a home, deep meaning and reverence for our surroundings:

A Home for the Soul: A Guide for Dwelling with Spirit and Imagination by Anthony Lawlor, 1997.

• By a woman who lived with the Amish and wrote of her fascinating experiences:

Plain and Simple and *Everyday Sacred: A Woman's Journey Home* by Sue Bender.

CHAPTER 5 — STAGES

• Ideas about old persons as "ancestors" who bear society's cultural memory and traditions:

The Force of Character and the Lasting Life by James Hillman, 1999.

• To help develop simple, deep pleasures of food, friends, family, home, and intimacy with nature:

The Soul of Sex by Thomas Moore, 1998.

• A good book for exploring each stage of relational development:

Keeping the Love You Find: A Guide for Singles by Harville Hendrix.

- An excellent book written for parents, using Imago theory:
  Giving the Love that Heals by Harville Hendrix and Helen Hunt.

CHAPTER 6 — WAGES

- An invitation for life to be less arduous and more delightful with understanding of the emerging science of complexity and its application to organizations – required reading for all who want to create life-supportive and life-sustaining forms:
  A Simpler Way by Margaret Wheatley and Myron Kellner-Rogers, 1996.

- Lots of statistics about women, earning power, and the wage gap:
  Megatrends for Women: From Liberation to Leadership by Patricia Aburdene and John Naisbitt, 1992.

- A book of daily readings promoting self-worth:
  Simple Abundance: A Daybook of Comfort and Joy by Sarah Ban Breathnach, 1995.

- *Manifest Your Destiny: The Nine Spiritual Principles for Getting Everything You Want* by Wayne W. Dyer, 1997.

CHAPTER 7 — SAGES

- A book that normalizes aging and gives hope to women past menopause:
  Old Age by Helen Luke, 1987.

- A transformational journey into the ancient stories of Odysseus, creating a map for your personal myth. Athena, as muse, provides a good working model for the Possible Woman:
  The Hero and the Goddess by Jean Houston, 1992.

• Health and happiness through five Aloha qualities (patience, connection, pleasantness, modesty, and tenderness):

The Pleasure Prescription by Paul Pearsall, 1996.

• A wakeup call for the reinvention of industry for a healthy population on a thriving planet for the next generations:

Mid-Course Correction by Ray C. Anderson, 1998.

• Understanding nature's model for sustaining life on Earth:

Biomimicry: Innovation Inspired by Nature by Janine M. Benyus, 1997.

• Native American wisdom that's practical for us today:

Daughters of Copperwoman by Ann Cameron, 1987.

• A helpful book for understanding quantum theory and the physics of consciousness – the quantum self is a free and responsive self, ultimately reflecting the world of nature:

The Quantum Self: Human Nature and Consciousness Defined by the New Physics by Danah Zohar, 1990.

• These books from the author of *He, She, We,* and *Inner Work* are among my favorites and are helpful in understanding masculinity and femininity:

Owning Your Own Shadow, 1991, and *Femininity Lost and Regained*, 1990, by Robert Johnson.

• A mind-stretching book telling us that we are far more connected than we ever dreamed:

The Holographic Universe by Michael Talbot, 1991.

BIBLIOGRAPHY

Arriens, Angeles. *The Four-Fold Way: Walking the Paths of the Warrior, Teacher, Healer, and Visionary.* Harper, 1993.

Bolen, Jean Shinoda. *Goddesses in Everywoman: A New Psychology of Women.* Harper Colophon, 1984.

Cameron, Julia. *The Artist's Way: A Spiritual Path to Higher Creativity.* J. P. Tarcher, 1992.

Campbell, Joseph. *The Hero with a Thousand Faces.* Princeton University Press, 1990.

Capra, Fritzjof. *The Web of Life: A New Scientific Understanding of Living Systems.* Doubleday, 1996.

Hendrix, Harville. *Getting the Love You Want: A Guide for Couples.* Henry Holt and Company, 1988.

_____. *Keeping the Love You Find: A Guide for Singles.* Pocket Books, 1992.

_____ and Helen Hunt. *Giving the Love that Heals: A Guide for Parents.* Pocket Books, 1997.

Houston, Jean. *Life Force: The Psychohistorical Recovery of the Self.* Quest Books, 1993.

_____, *The Possible Human: A Course in Enhancing Your Physical, Mental, and Creative Abilities.* Jeremy P. Tarcher, Inc., 1982.

_____. *The Search for the Beloved: Journeys in Mythology and Sacred Psychology.* Jeremy P. Tarcher, Inc., 1987.

James, Muriel. *It's Never Too Late to Be Happy: The Psychology of Self Re-Parenting.* Addison-Wesley, 1985.

Karlsen, Carol F. *The Devil in the Shape of a Woman: Witchcraft in Colonial New England.* W. W. Norton and Company, 1987.

Luke, Helen. *The Way of Woman: Awakening the Perennial Feminine.* Bantam, 1992.

MacLain, Paul. *"On the Evolution of Three Mentalities,"* in *New Dimensions in Psychiatry: A World View,* Vol. 2, Wiley, 1977.

Montague, Ashley. *The Natural Superiority of Women,* Collier Books, 1972.

_____. *Growing Young.* Rbhp Trade Group, 1989.

Pearsall, Paul. *The Heart's Code: Tapping the Wisdom and Power of Our Heart Energy.* Broadway Books, 1998.

Roberts, Cokie. *We Are Our Mothers' Daughters.* Wm. Morrow & Co., 1998.

Shlain, Leonard. *The Alphabet Versus the Goddess: The Conflict Between Word and Image.* Viking, 1998.

Verny, Thomas, et al. *The Secret Life of the Unborn Child.* Delta Books, 1994 (reprint edition).

ABOUT THE AUTHOR

Marjorie R. Barlow was born in 1929 and grew up on a cotton farm in the Texas panhandle. She earned her high school diploma in 1944 and in 1947, at age eighteen, she received a bachelor's degree in Business Administration from Texas College of Arts & Industries, Kingsville. She married after graduation, had four children, Anna, Michael, Kaye, and Edward, and taught school while her husband completed his doctorate in theoretical physics.

Widowed at age 33 with four small children to support, she worked as a church organist and day school principal and returned to school, earning a master's degree in Psychology from Texas A & I in 1966. She married her second husband, college professor Dr. Paul Barlow, in 1964. Their daughter Cynthia was born in 1970.

She entered the counseling profession in 1966, first as a high school counselor, then as a marriage and family therapist and executive director of Kleberg County (Texas) Family Guidance Services. She received her Ph.D. in Education in 1978 from University of Nebraska-Lincoln shortly before her fiftieth birthday.

Currently, she maintains a private practice as a Licensed Professional Counselor and Licensed Marriage and Family Therapist and works as a consultant to corporations and other groups on relationships and the dialogical process, helping to identify and develop women as leaders, facilitate diversity awareness, and support sustainability for the Earth. She also is a resource consultant to the Young Presidents' Organization, a Certified Clinical Imago Relationship Therapist, and a Certified Presenter for Getting the Love You Want Workshops.

Marjorie Barlow is the author of two books, *Couples Night Out* (1996) and *The Possible Woman* (1999) and is working on a third, *Wisdom in the Workplace*.

Her husband returned to school after his retirement from university teaching in 1995 and is creating a new career as a Registered Play Therapist. They enjoy working together helping marriages, children, and family relationships and a life that includes work, exercise, meditation, good conversation, study, and spiritual stretching.

For information on Marjorie Barlow's seminars and public appearances, contact:

Barlow Family Services
728 Elizabeth #4
Corpus Christi, TX 78404
Voice: 361-882-4356
Fax: 361-884-9048
E-mail: MarjBarlow@aol.com